Your guide to the
ALEXANDER
TECHNIQUE

To my mother and father

Acknowledgements

My grateful love and thanks to Inge Henderson, my first teacher who undoubtedly saved my life and opened up a whole new wonderful world; to Gwyneth Cole and Ann Battye, my colleagues who have sustained me over many years; to my editors Liz Knights and Elfreda Powell, with whom it has been a joy to work; to Alec McCowen, a good friend and excellent pupil, for his Foreword; to David Ball for help with the manuscript; to those of my RADA students who helped with the photographs; and most gratefully of all to Dr Wilfred Barlow and my valued friend Marjory Alexander Barlow who should really have written this book.

J.G.

Your guide to the
ALEXANDER TECHNIQUE

JOHN GRAY

VICTOR GOLLANCZ
LONDON

First published in Great Britain 1990
by Victor Gollancz Ltd
First paperback edition published 1994
by Victor Gollancz
This edition published 1998
by Victor Gollancz
An imprint of the Cassell Group
Wellington House, 125 Strand,
London WC2R 0BB

A catalogue record for this book is
available from the British Library
ISBN 0 575 06713 6

Photoset in Great Britain by
Rowland Phototypesetting Ltd, Bury St Edmunds, Suffolk
and manufactured in Great Britain by
Butler & Tanner Ltd, Frome and London

98 99   10 9 8 7 6 5 4 3 2 1

Contents

PART TWO: THE INTERMEDIATE LESSONS

I love the Alexander Technique.

It has corrected my posture, improved my health, and changed my life.

When I was playing the psychiatrist, Dr Martin Dysart, in Peter Shaffer's play *Equus* I became increasingly aware of tense and aching shoulder-blades, and arthritic pains in my hands. Unhappy Dr Dysart felt imprisoned in his life and work, and to play him I had adopted – all too easily – a physically defeated posture. During the year's run in London, this carried over into my own life. I was a prematurely stooped old man.

I mentioned the arthritic pains to my doctor. He astonished me by saying that these pains were probably related to tension in my neck and suggested that I think about the Alexander Principle.

My friend John Gray had been a pupil of Wilfred Barlow, the chief practitioner of the Alexander Principle in London. He was now a qualified teacher himself, and, whenever I saw him, would nag me gently about my bad posture and tell me that I needed a course of lessons. He also said that it would help me mentally – adding intolerantly, 'More than any analyst!'

I decided to take him up on it, and, before going on a holiday to India, I had a two-week course of lessons with John.

It was while I was in India that I found out that it worked. A group of us had a long drive on a dreadful bumpy road in a jeep from Darjeeling to Kalimpong. On the way home, I was sitting in front and I thought the journey would wreck my back – as well as my nerves and digestion. Everyone was in great discomfort. But I started to practise the Alexander Principle, and at the end of the long journey I was as fresh as a daisy and led the company in a rowdy sing-song.

The Alexander Principle has helped me mentally also. I am not tall, and it makes me feel taller.

I find that even in a tense or difficult situation, it is easy to remember the basic Alexander instructions, and this has made it easier to deal with the trouble. You may as well be nervous with a relaxed neck as with a tense neck – and the relaxed neck may lead to further physical and mental relaxation.

It has also helped me professionally, and I have delighted in the novelty of being praised for the way I stand or sit. It is better than being praised for my acting.

If you work at it, the Alexander Principle will work for you.

Foreword by Alec McCowen
CBE

For USE almost can change the stamp of Nature,
And either curb the devil, or throw him out,
With wondrous potency.

                        William Shakespeare

Introduction: where fools rush in

With the growing popularity and interest in the Alexander Technique recently, there have been any number of books written on the subject. The best of these are very useful, some are rather specialised, others are written from a restricted personal viewpoint and are of limited value, and some are positively misleading.

Alexander's own books were for a long time out-of-print but are now again available and will continue to be the source to which we must frequently return to refresh ourselves from the original knowledge and inspiration of the technique. However, many people find them difficult to read and even more so to understand. The style is undeniably old-fashioned and wordy, though with perseverance and further knowledge of the work, one realises just how good the books are and how very difficult it is to write about this subject.

The Alexander process is essentially a unifying one with many different areas interconnecting, and so it is not easy to break it down into separate sections. On the other hand, it is too easy when describing the technique to start at any given point and ramble on, veering off in any direction, as any particular aspect can have a bearing on any other, and so the problems of being systematic and fluent are daunting. It is a difficult subject but I have tried to illustrate these connecting and interacting areas, without complicating matters more than is absolutely necessary, and whilst describing the essential, basic procedures in the learning process and retaining a semblance of structure, I have introduced a number of ideas that seek to improve an understanding of the Alexander Technique. The basic essentials are rarely described in print and, in some cases, when attempted, quite inaccurately, often with too much attention given to how the technique will help and not enough to emphasising the amount and nature of the work needed to be done before being able to apply it.

My own, probably foolhardy, reasons for venturing into print are numerous and varied, but mainly to try to answer the cry: 'But what is it all about? What happens in the lessons? How do I learn the technique? Why is it all so mysterious? We're never told *what to do* to learn the method!' People still ask these questions, however much they might have read on the subject. Indeed, some of the books on the teaching, often by journalists or those who are not qualified teachers, only serve to bewilder and even misinform.

A further aim of the book has been to eliminate some of the unnecessary mystery that seems to surround the subject; to keep to a basic approach that includes the essential elements of learning and teaching, describing the procedures involved. This does not have to be as complicated or recondite as has previously been suggested, but nor should what is a difficult discipline be oversimplified so as to mislead anyone who might wish to learn it.

In the first flush of enthusiasm experienced when having lessons, pupils naturally try to communicate their zeal to their nearest and dearest. Nothing is so off-putting as an apparent excess of enthusiasm, proselytising or fanaticism, and nothing so dangerous as the proverbial 'little learning'. One of the reasons why so much of the written material in the past was inadequate is that it was so personal, either describing the individual's experiences in the lessons or how the work was able to be applied with dramatic effect. Every pupil will have different, and often vivid, experiences with a good teacher, and they are usually valid and useful, but describing the Alexander Technique only from this highly personal and limited viewpoint does not do it justice. These new experiences are often so remarkable that it is an understandable temptation to want to share them, but as there are almost as many different kinds of experience as there are pupils of the technique this can be very confusing, and to describe such happenings might not be at all enlightening or relevant to that particular reader or listener, even though there will be certain experiences common to many pupils.

There are many routes up a mountain and many ways to the truth and we must beware of suggesting that our own is the only one, so it is on a more general level that I am about to embark on this dangerous course: hoping to show how the individual can find his or her own way forward and get his own rewards in many different and individual experiences.

There are certain basic elements essential to a proper knowledge and understanding of the technique and it is these I shall try to describe, for without these it can easily become just another approach to body mechanics, a 'body awareness' method, or a 'fringe' approach to problems, and not, as I see it, the most important means of self-discovery and way of guiding one's own personal evolutionary journey through the difficult and complex experiences of modern living. Too often these basics are ignored at the expense of a complete view of what the technique can allow and help accomplish; too narrow an approach is presented, which, whilst perfectly valid in itself, will limit the individual pupil in finding out for himself the widest possible implications and applications of 'the work', as Alexander called it.

It might reasonably be asked why I think I am a suitable person to describe this most important discipline and means of coping with life, when there are no doubt many others wiser and more experienced who have not dared, so I will try to justify my efforts.

Having been trained as a teacher of the technique by Marjory Alexander Barlow and Dr Wilfred Barlow I feel particularly privileged. Marjory is the niece of Alexander, or 'F.M.' as he was generally known, and lived with him, was trained by him and worked with him for many years, so I feel pleasantly close to the origins of the work. Dr Barlow, her husband, is the leading medical exponent of the teaching, has done much of the scientific research into it, and is largely responsible for setting it on a respectable footing in the eyes of scientists and enlightened scholars. So I am lucky in having the combination of close associations with the roots of the work and with the more recent scientific 'back-up'.

In the past I have occasionally tried to write about the technique and have realised some of the difficulties and pitfalls, but at the back of my mind there has always been the idea of a 'basic approach', and the more I read about the Technique the more I realise that we are often getting away from this basic approach. With the training of more and more teachers, some inadequately supervised, the word is spreading rapidly. So this is a time to beware of dissipating the important truths and matter in the work, and a time to gather up one's thoughts and views on the essential elements in the teaching.

With more than twenty years' experience in the work, many of them as a teacher in varied areas, the Alexander Institute, a medical practice, and the Royal Academy of Dramatic Art, perhaps this is an opportune moment to be bold, take stock, and venture into print. I am no longer in the first flush of fanatical enthusiasm, but nor so ancient as to find writing a chore, nor in the position of finding myself with nobody around with whom I can check original facts, discoveries, and sources of information. Whilst I shall no doubt continue to gain wider and more valuable experience as a teacher, I have had sufficient time in the work to be aware of the difficulties and realise the importance of sticking to the vital ingredients. I like to think that it is a combination of experience and freshness.

Over the years I have been making notes, and from the start I jotted down the important ideas and points of interest suggested by my own teachers so that I would not forget to include them in my teaching. This book will therefore cover what I consider to be the essential pure truths of the work as passed on to me by my teachers, along with how to apply these ideas in the practical procedures involved in learning, applying, and teaching the technique.

Whilst there is no substitute for actual lessons, reading about the subject can help. My early experiences in my lessons gave me tremendous relief from pain and paralysis, so I was lucky in that I knew something beneficial was happening, but for a long time I didn't understand why or how. Maybe, at that stage, I was in such a mess that I was incapable of hearing or understanding, or perhaps my teacher, who literally saved my life, was not articulate enough, but it is certain that reading about the technique helped me enormously. I began to understand it on another level, with my brain as well as my body. My improved state made me want to find out why and how it worked, and written material allowed me to clarify my ideas as to the means whereby the technique helped.

In theory you can teach yourself the principle, and a number of people claim to have done so. Certainly F.M. had no help other than his own resources when working it all out. But for us lesser mortals, who are not touched with his genius, expert instruction is essential and the right books can be a big help in understanding and knowing what to expect from our lessons. We need to avoid pitfalls and digressions. Good tuition can speed up the changing process involved, and careful guidance can check this process and forestall time-wasting experiences.

Aldous Huxley maintained that the Alexander Technique was the most difficult of all disciplines, as you have, in the final analysis, no one else to rely on but yourself. You do not have an outside agent, guru or god to guide you when you are on your own as you mostly are. Alexander himself was constantly telling his pupils that he could not do the work for them. It is a journey into the unknown with little reference to past experience. Good written material can complement a good teacher.

What is the Alexander Technique?

The Alexander Technique is a process of psycho-physical re-education: by inhibiting automatic habitual responses it allows you to eliminate old habits of reaction and mis-use of the body and, through more reliable sensory appreciation, brings about improved use and a more appropriate means of reaction.

As teachers we are often asked what we do and what the technique is. The explanation given above is quite a mouthful and tends to shut people up, so it is often better to stick to simpler terms like 'kinaesthetic re-education', 'a way of teaching you to react more appropriately', or 'a way of eliminating unnecessary tension in the way we move, react and use our bodies'. Even these terms only tell part of the story, and usually elicit the response, 'Oh, like Yoga!' Sometimes the reaction is, 'Oh yes, it's all about relaxing isn't it?' or, more alarmingly once, 'Oh yes, I know all about that, it's bone-stretching isn't it?'

Sometimes it is simpler to say what it is not. It is not only about good posture, or 'relaxing', 'standing up straight', or a series of exercises. Nor is it only about being expertly manipulated. It is not a therapy or a treatment. It includes elements of the above but to describe it as such is to touch upon only its minor aspects, to limit it severely and to undersell it.

Simple, everyday activities can create all kinds of tension

Unnecessary tension

Most of us are making a great deal of unnecessary tension most of the time in the way we use our bodies, even when we think we are relaxed. Indeed 'relaxation' to many people suggests a state of collapse or 'flopping about', which tends to encourage flaccid muscles, often a distortion of the structure, and a great deal of harmful pressure into various areas and joints. It is probably better not to think in terms of 'relaxing', but of returning to a 'balanced state of rest', in which the body is well-aligned, with a desirable combination of freedom and stability present in the right areas. We must have tension but it must be the right kind of tension, in fact it is better to think of it as 'tone'. If we have no

'Relaxing' is too often merely collapsing

tension we fall down, but often there is the wrong kind of tension in the wrong areas, instead of muscle tone in the right areas. It is quite common, for example, to be very collapsed in the lower back area but very tense in the shoulders; the main supporting muscles in the back and abdomen which are constantly at work lack tone, and the secondary muscles, which should only be brought into play for specific jobs, become overworked. So, often the re-education process is concerned with respreading the workload in the body – releasing unnecessary tension and encouraging desirable tone through improved use.

The fashionable slump

It is often the case that we have been making a great deal of unnecessary tension from a very early age. I believe it is nowadays recognised that, as children, learning to speak can interfere with the free poise and balance of the head: things can go wrong at as early a stage as that. Then, of course, we imitate our parents and schoolfellows, collapse over desks all day long, bored to tears in lessons or at work, or we are told to 'sit up straight' or 'stand up properly', and people's ideas of 'straight' and 'properly' are very odd. Maybe we assume a fashionable stance like the punks or adopt the adolescent 'slump', or at work we could be hunched over a typewriter or twisted over a machine for years on end. We all have traumas, difficult situations to cope with or worrying periods in our lives, and these can set up a great many harmful tension patterns in the body. Unless we know how to release this tension and return to a balanced state of rest, we can easily incorporate some of it into our automatic, habitual way of using our body and carry around in our physical development harmful response patterns to situations long since past – almost as though we are carrying around a whole lifetime's problems in our poor weary bodies.

There are many theories as to why things go wrong. One is that modern diet encourages greater strength and growth, but modern lifestyles produce less physical stimulation than in previous years – and often the wrong sort of stimulation, in that we tend either to rush around leading madly busy lives, or sit for hours at desks or cooped up in cars. At the same time we are being over-stimulated mentally by sophisticated modern urban living, so that there is a lack of harmony between brain and body. Alexander maintained that we have lost our instinctive good use of the body through the evolutionary process; others maintain that we lose it very early on in childhood.

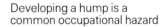

Developing a hump is a common occupational hazard

Patterns of mis-use

For reasons like these, and no doubt many thousands of others, unless we are particularly lucky, we tend over a period of time to develop a great deal of stress and strain, wear and tear, and a very complex pattern of body mis-use, often allied to entrenched habits of thought and reaction. Although it might be nice to know how we came to be in this mess, this complicated pattern of mis-use, it is not that important; the really encouraging factor is that we can do something about it. We are taught to do most things in this life but not how to use ourselves well. We just hope that things will work out all right and that the instinctive or copied patterns will see us through – so why not? As the body is not designed to work in the way that most people are forcing it into, if we give it a chance to work in the natural balanced manner for which it was designed, it actually prefers this way and begins to function more efficiently. Alas, after a certain age most of us never give the body this chance, but force it back into the old ways in everything that we are doing.

The body, however, is remarkably resilient and, considering what most people are doing to it, can go on functioning well for surprisingly long. Nevertheless, these days most of us seem to reach a point at which we realise that all is not well. If we don't develop a bad back, we might get tension headaches; if not those, then perhaps a frozen shoulder, or housemaid's knee, flat feet, tennis elbow, digestive problems, inability to sleep, or just more general problems of irritability, clumsiness, accident-proneness, lethargy or tiredness. Such problems, and many, many others, are frequently caused by mis-using ourselves or are certainly aggravated by mis-use, so the analysis of a person's use of himself or herself is an area of diagnosis which should be taken into account, though usually it isn't. At best most doctors can only see the more obvious manifestations of mis-use in their patients: perhaps one shoulder is much higher than the other, or the patient has an excessively curved spine, but often the doctor cannot see the subtler forms and can rarely tell the patients what to do about themselves even if he can recognise the problem. So here is another area that a skilled teacher should be able to deal

Sitting badly

with: how to use our bodies for maximum efficiency of functioning.

When we talk of 'use' or 'mis-use', all we mean is how we involve our bodies in the things we do: how we stand, perhaps with legs braced, or more on one leg than the other; how we sit, maybe with knees crossed or maybe collapsing in the lower back area; how we walk and move, which muscles are involved to what degree and in what combination; how misaligned the body is; how we throw our weight forward when standing, or sideways when walking; whether the head is pulled back constantly or worn over to one side. The harmful pressures and strain on the structure of the body caused by such ways of moving, acting and reacting are the results of such 'mis-use' and interfere with efficient functioning, but if a person is well-aligned, with the body in a good state of balance and tone when either still or in movement, with the maximum freedom combined with stability, we consider this to be 'good use' resulting usually in unimpaired functioning.

The term 'psycho-physical' might be rather off-putting to some people, but the Alexander Technique is essentially a holistic approach to problems, unlike conventional medicine and other methods of dealing with our ills which often try to separate the two sides of the self into the 'physical' and the 'mental', though fortunately this is becoming less acceptable. Everybody knows how much more in control of situations we are when we 'feel well', how much better the world seems after a good night's sleep, how much less fraught we feel when things go smoothly. Every stimulus involves the brain and the reaction to that stimulus more often than not is an outward, physical, bodily reaction. Many of these stimuli are at a low level of consciousness and many of our reactions are reflex, but both areas can be brought under control and, instead of being slaves to our habits, we can begin to master them, habits of thought as well as physical responses, though we often cannot separate the two.

This is easier said than done, as many of the things we are doing to ourselves, the patterns we bring into play throughout the whole structure of the body, are unconscious, automatic, immediate and deeply habitual. We seem to be conditioned from an early age into responding instantaneously without thinking, being constantly exhorted to 'hurry up', 'get on with it' and so on. Yet many of these activities will be carried out inefficiently and with a great deal of unnecessary tension, strain and distortion of the structure, with muscles often used in a very unbalanced, haphazard way, constantly reinforcing old harmful patterns that have been built up over the years. In new, difficult or complex activities and situations, we might not only be reinforcing the old bad habits but adding on an extra layer or two of compensatory tension in our effort to overcome our inefficient functioning, building up yet more, new bad habits. And so, trying to catch this moment of reaction, the instant when the stimulus is acted upon, will be of first importance to pupils if they wish to bring a little more conscious control to bear over the way they are responding, so that in time they will be less likely to be perpetuating old bad habits in the use of themselves.

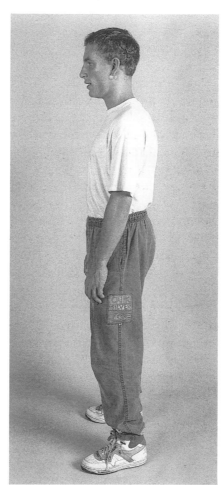

The military's idea of standing straight as against the easier, more balanced Alexander version

F.M.'s story

For a proper understanding of the Alexander Technique, and for those who are unfamiliar with it, a knowledge of Frederick Matthias Alexander and how he came to work it out is essential. The story has often been told, in particular by F.M. himself in the third of his four books called *The Use of the Self* and so this section can be skipped by those already acquainted with it.

Alexander was born in Tasmania in 1869, the eldest and rather sickly child in a large family, who lived on a large remote property. He could rarely, if ever, have gone to the theatre, but for some strange reason he wanted to become an actor or reciter, probably due to the influence of his schoolmaster who instilled into him a love of Shakespeare.

As a young man he went off to Melbourne to train to become an actor, not any old actor but a 'Great Shakespearean Actor', working at other jobs to support himself. After a while he started to give recitals, as was the fashion of the time, of 'dramatic and humorous pieces'. Quickly he gained a measure of success and was well on the way to becoming this 'Great Shakespearean Actor' when a recurring setback led him to the first big turning point in his life: during an important engagement his voice became hoarse and finally disappeared. This, for an actor, was of course a disaster. Off he went to a doctor who suggested various conventional remedies such as throat sprays and resting the voice – all right as far as they went but no use when he started reciting again, as back came the old problems. Then there were suggestions of an operation, but as no really good reason could be given for this he said 'no thank you' and went away to think about it.

'There must be something different that I am doing when acting, or reciting, than when I am speaking ordinarily', he thought, 'as I don't have this trouble with ordinary speaking. If I could find out the difference between what I am doing to myself in these two activities perhaps I could find out the cause of my voice trouble.' And so began a long period of detailed analysis of how he was carrying out various activities with particular attention to speaking and reciting.

He arranged mirrors in front and to the side of himself so that he could observe exactly how he was doing these things and he began to discover what was most noticeable of all when reciting: how he

F.M. Alexander

was mis-using himself. It became obvious that he was doing curious things particularly with his neck, head and trunk. As he sucked in air to speak he raised his chest at the same time as pulling his head backwards and downwards, thereby depressing the larynx, and having raised his chest and interfered with the balance of the head he had also shortened his spine and narrowed his back, thereby also interfering with his breathing, not to mention tensing the buttocks and legs and pressing down into his feet – his way of misinterpreting the instruction to 'take hold of the stage with the feet' suggested by a famous actor of the day. In fact he had created just about as much tension as he possibly could throughout the whole structure of the body.

'Well,' he thought. 'I don't do all that when speaking ordinarily, or at least not so obviously, perhaps this is the cause of the trouble, so I'd better try and do the opposite: keep my head up, not raise the chest, not suck in the breath, shorten the spine, etc.' However, because his whole idea of acting or reciting had been built up by creating these patterns, when he didn't do so it felt peculiar and wrong. He also found that the mental decision to recite instantly triggered off all these old patterns. Some of these habits were no doubt allied to the 'Grand Manner' and declamatory style prevailing in the Victorian theatre when the actor's voice had to fill a large auditorium. When he became carried away by a particularly dramatic or emotional passage he would immediately forget to 'do the opposite', and back would come all the old habits and feelings associated in his mind with acting, and he would be in just as big a mess as he was before trying to sort himself out. In fact trying to 'do something' to sort himself out was getting him into a thorough muddle. What he needed was to STOP DOING certain things to himself.

He realised that he had better go back to the very beginning, to the instant when the stimulus to open his mouth and recite was triggered off in his brain. If he were to react to this stimulus in the old way he would once again reinforce all the old habits, patterns and feelings associated in his mind and body with acting and probably go on to lose his voice again. If he could learn to 'inhibit' this automatic, habitual reaction, perhaps he could learn to bring about an improved reaction, through using his intelligence, and not interfere with his vocal mechanism. So he started to apply this idea of 'inhibition' and he used the word in its original sense before it had attained any psychological Freudian sense of suppressing feelings or being inhibited. Indeed he used it deliberately because words like 'stopping off' or 'preventing' a reaction had, he thought, suggestions of rigidity and he didn't want to replace the old harmful response with a new, probably harmful one, i.e., going rigid, but merely to withhold consent from his old habitual response so that he could give himself a moment's pause in which he could eventually choose a new reasonable response.

After inhibiting he then found he had to use his intelligence to work out what constituted a reasonable response, and as he was most obviously interfering in the neck, head and back areas of his body he began by attending to these. The interference with the balance of the head seemed to be because he was over-involving the neck muscles, i.e., he had stiffened his neck, so he thought, 'I must relax or release my neck. If I stiffen the neck I pull my head back and down, so I'd better direct it to do the opposite, i.e., "go forward and up", and as I at the same time shorten the spine and narrow the back as I take a breath I'd better direct the back to "lengthen and widen".'

These directions or orders were at this point mainly to prevent him going back into the old bad habits, guiding orders to stop things getting worse, but as these old harmful habits were long-standing and deeply-seated, and in many cases allied to reflex muscle patterns, he found that initially and for some time he had to get used to this way of attending to himself and not care too much about carrying out various activities or trying to apply these ideas too directly. He had to set down quite clearly in his mind the new track along which he was eventually going to go, without being lured off into the harmful sidetracks or old ways, which still felt largely right.

This awareness of the neck, head and back he called the 'Primary Control' of the body. The attention to the free poise and balance of the head he found to be particularly important; if he could prevent the interference here he could nip in the bud a whole sequence of harmful results, and as the Primary Control became operative, there was a marked improvement in co-ordination, sensory awareness, reaction and general functioning.

As this new pattern of thought became established, he became, after some time, more secure in his attention to the Primary Control and through this new means he could bring about an improvement in his reactions and functioning. He would give himself a stimulus to carry out some activity, perhaps move or speak, 'inhibit' or say 'no' to his immediate, old, automatic, habitual response to this stimulus, project his orders to his neck, head and back, and whilst continuing to keep these orders in mind and continuing to inhibit his old reaction, then allow the movement or activity to take place, accomplishing it without over-involving the neck muscles, interfering with the poise and balance of the head which in turn allowed him not to shorten and narrow the back.

In many activities this felt very odd as it was so different from what he was used to, but he could see in the mirror that it actually looked better. He wasn't creating all the tension and strain throughout the body, was maintaining more height, and most important for him, was functioning better in that he wasn't losing his voice. So he realised that, if he wanted to continue to improve, he had to a large extent to disregard his feelings, as these were too strongly associated with the old harmful ways; and he realised that he must learn to trust the new means of observing himself, inhibiting his old habitual responses, and directing the body in this new way. After a while the new ways began to feel less and less peculiar and insecure, indeed eventually the old ways began actually to feel wrong, as the new 'Ordered State' began to be associated with a more reliable sensory mechanism.

After continuing as an actor for some time as well as a teacher of these new ideas, he went to Sydney to become the director of the Sydney Operatic and Dramatic Conservatorium. Here he was teaching young actors about voice and speech and to his surprise he found that many of them were also interfering with this neck/head/back relationship, not always in exactly the same way as he had been doing but in rather similar ways, so he continued to apply these ideas to his teaching and came to the notice of an eminent physician in Sydney, a Doctor McKay, who was impressed by his work and thought he ought to be practising in London. With this doctor's encouragement he came to London in 1904, although slightly reluctantly as it was a big step for a young man in those days. Winning £750 by investing £5 on a tip for a double in the Newmarket Handicap and the Australia Cup at odds of 150–1 before he left no doubt seemed like a good omen. His great love of horses, from his childhood, and of gambling to some extent, stayed with him all his life.

His introductions to various medical men in London fell largely on deaf ears, except one to a Dr Scanes Spicer, a leading ear, nose and throat specialist. He had a large practice amongst the theatrical profession and started sending his patients to F.M., so almost from the start Alexander was teaching such people as Henry Irving, Lillie Langtry and Herbert Beerbohm Tree. He taught a great many famous people including such writers as Aldous Huxley and Bernard Shaw, who both wrote about the technique, politicians and statesmen like Sir Stafford Cripps, Ben Gurion, and the Earl of Lytton, Viceroy of India, Archbishops Temple and Lang, John Dewey the American educational philosopher, and many musicians including Sir Adrian Boult. Over the years the technique became quite well-known amongst a small élite circle and in the 1920s and 30s it became quite fashionable to go and be 'Alexandered', but as he was the only teacher it was not widely known. His brother, A. R. Alexander, who had taught with him in Australia, joined him in London and F.M. took on a couple of female assistants, Ethel Webb and Irene Tasker, but still he was reluctant to train new teachers, maintaining that he couldn't be sure of them making a living and he did not want to be responsible for training people in something by which they could not support themselves.

Amongst those doctors who knew about the technique there was a feeling that it should be incorporated into medical training, and there were letters to the leading medical journals suggesting this, and pointing out that here was a whole area of diagnosis that was being ignored: how the way we use our bodies affects their functioning, hence mis-use prevents efficient functioning. Although the medical profession is now, in great numbers, finally coming round to realising this – due largely to the efforts and research of Dr Wilfred Barlow, plus the support of a number of eminent medical people such as Professor Nikolaos Tinbergen who devoted much of his Laureate Oration to the technique when receiving his Nobel Prize in Medicine in 1973 – it is still largely ignorant in this area.

The training of Alexander teachers in groups finally started in 1931, by which time F.M. was in his sixties, but then the Second World War broke out and every night bombers were flying over his school for young children in Kent, so it was thought best that he be shipped off to the USA with his school for the duration of the war. Both he and his brother had taught regularly in the States for many years. Also he had made some rather insulting remarks about the German educational system in his last book *The Universal Constant in Living* and was no doubt on the lists for elimination if ever the Nazis arrived. After the war he had to sue the South African government for libel in a case which he won, and then again he won in the Appeal Court. By this time, however, he was an old man though he continued to teach regularly – even after working on himself and recovering completely from a stroke when he was 78 – until his death in 1955, aged 86.

His niece Marjory Barlow had kept the flag flying during the war. When most of the other teachers were away, she was the only teacher still working in London, and on F.M.'s return in 1943 handed over her practice to him.

The main point of F. M.'s story is that in some way or other most of us have to go through a similar process of discovery. Fortunately, with his experience, and as teaching becomes more expert, our way forward does not have to be so tortuous, long-winded or experimental as that which F.M. had to travel. We have to learn to recognise and observe our problems, learn to inhibit old responses that force the body constantly back into harmful patterns that aggravate old problems and cause new ones to develop, and then learn to order or direct ourselves in such a way as to allow for a new 'means whereby' we can improve, change and fulfil our greater potential. The essential elements of the Technique can therefore be considered to be Inhibition, Direction or Ordering, and Working on Oneself, in order to apply it. Anything less would be missing out some vital aspect.

Part One

The Early Lessons

The pupil/teacher relationship is of great importance if there is to be a fruitful outcome to the first course of lessons. Some pupils set great store by their teachers and become fiercely loyal, possibly because they have tried so many other fields for their needs and found them wanting. Some pupils are highly suspicious and virtually challenge the teacher to 'do something with this mess', imagining the lessons to be some kind of treatment or miraculous answer to their problems, or perhaps they confront the teacher with an all-too-obvious boredom, especially if they have been sent by their parents or spouse and told that this is 'just what they need'. More often than not the pupil will develop a close personal relationship with the teacher quite quickly, but this should be kept strictly professional and the pupil should not become over-reliant on the teacher, as it makes for problems when he or she has to continue without the back-up of regular lessons. Pupils by then should not feel abandoned but confident enough to cope on their own. Some of Alexander's early students saw him in a hallowed light and, when he turned out to be as human as the next man in many ways, they tended to resent this, rather as children do when they find that their parents are no longer the centre of the universe.

Initially the wise teacher will spend some time getting to know and make friends with pupils and will perhaps need to listen to their problems, though too much analysis in this area can be a waste of time and irrelevant to the teaching, and it is sensible to try to get pupils on to an Alexander 'wavelength' as early as possible, rather than the teacher being seduced into playing the listener and being cast into some preconceived role that pupils think they need.

The teacher will start to observe and analyse the pupils' use of their body from the outset. He or she will be able to tell a good deal from how pupils enter the room, make their greeting, listen, sit down or get up. Although at this first meeting pupils might well be nervous, shy or suspicious, this will be a fair indication of how they often react in such situations.

Perhaps the teacher will chat in a friendly fashion, getting to know a little more about the pupil but still observing how he or she speaks, listens, reacts and is seated. Did the pupil get into the chair by stiffening the neck and pulling back the head, or hunching the shoulders and sticking out the bottom; has he or she now slumped down and crossed the knees, or is the pupil self-consciously trying to hold him- or herself erect, creating a lot of tension in the front of the chest by trying to 'sit up straight'? After being put at ease the pupil will probably have lapsed into certain familiar patterns which the teacher will note and, if it is thought helpful at this stage, the teacher may point out some of the more obvious ones, though taking care to emphasise that the pupil can as yet do little about them.

Some teachers prefer a more formal consultation, and, if they have the expert medical knowledge, might examine the pupil in some detail. Certainly the wise teacher will check the pupil's medical history, particularly back problems. There are grids against which the pupil can be stood and other ways of measuring asymmetry and indications of mis-use, which are useful but not absolutely necessary. At this point, measuring the height of the pupil can also be interesting as many of them will grow noticeably taller during a course of lessons; the teacher will also suggest that comfortable clothes are worn.

Pupils might well be glad to know that they will not have to do very much in the lessons, that they are not about to undergo a rigorous physical training programme or series of exercises, though they will be unlikely to appreciate how difficult it can be to STOP DOING many of the things that are causing their problems, if there are any, or how difficult it can be merely to leave themselves alone to allow a necessary 'undoing' process to begin to take effect.

After some general remarks on what the technique is all about, what sort of programme is to be embarked upon, and what the pupil may expect from the lessons, the first important idea to be emphasised is that of inhibition.

Inhibition

Most pupils in their first lesson will have got into and out of a chair in some very uncoordinated fashion and, with the teacher's help, they might now perhaps examine and try a better way. The emphasis now will be on the point that the pupil must constantly 'inhibit' his old idea of getting into or out of the chair and leave himself alone, allowing the teacher with his or her hands to bring about one or two subtle adjustments to the pupil's stance. By getting the pupil to pay more attention to a new, improved *means* of sitting or standing and not be concerned with the end-result (or 'end-gaining'), a skilful teacher should be able to coax the pupil into a more coordinated state, with less habitual interference. By allowing the head to be more freely poised – which also allows for a more lengthened spine – and by getting the knees to bend or move away over the toes, in line with the feet, the pupil will have the experience of sitting or rising with far less effort than is usual. This experience of not reinforcing the old habits so strongly, of leaving oneself alone more and of being subtly helped by the teacher can be very novel and enlightening. The pupil can be made to appreciate the economy of effort and subtle connection throughout the structure that is naturally there when using the body well, and feel lighter and more lengthened. Equally one may feel so insecure and off balance when not allowed to rely on the old tension patterns that one might not yet like the new feeling. The pupil must then be reassured on this point, and it must be explained how one relies on tension, how the new ways will not necessarily feel better for a while, though in the early lessons most pupils will quite quickly experience pleasanter sensations.

Feelings of ease, lightness, well-being, lengthening and growing are common; however, some pupils, whilst they might be able to see in a mirror that they are changing – apparently growing, altering in shape or even functioning noticeably better in some areas – will not necessarily feel very different. Others might not look so different but can, from a very early stage, feel entirely different, less harassed and irritable, lighter and more energetic, more easily able to cope with various situations and areas of their lives. In some way the lessons should be beneficial to most people and generally in a number of areas and on several levels.

Having given the pupil the experience of carrying out an apparently simple movement in a more economic, efficient and beneficial way, the teacher might then try working on the pupil on a couch or table. This will be similar to an orthopaedic couch or refectory table approximately seven feet long by two feet six inches wide with a small amount of padding for comfort and roughly the height of a dining table, or whatever suits the teacher best.

The idea behind this type of work at this stage is to give the pupil the experience of undoing unnecessary tension and bringing about an improved connection throughout the structure, by the better relating of one part of the body to another. It is also the best way of conveying at an early stage the experience of a good 'balanced state of rest', but more of that later. If the teacher is at all skilled and has introduced the idea of Inhibition, which in this situation means refusing to react to the teacher's hands coaxing and manipulating the pupil into a better state, he or she should be able to give the pupil vivid experiences of being better coordinated and connected, lighter and easier. The pupil must not help, otherwise he would have a preconceived idea of what was required and if he knew that he probably would not need lessons; nor must he resist, as he would then make it difficult or impossible for the teacher to bring about any improvement.

A practical demonstration of what Inhibition means is useful at this stage as no amount of verbal explanation to some pupils allows them to be able to inhibit when the time comes to apply the idea. Almost always in an early lesson there will be a time when the pupil is asked to 'Sit down' or carry out some other act and will immediately 'jump to it'. It is a good idea to point out then just what he or she did and how he or she reacted without thinking. When working on the couch I suggest that pupils think to themselves, 'No, I am not going to react to the teacher's hands. "No" to helping, hindering, adjusting, collapsing, stiffening, fixing, flopping or making preparatory tension as he or she manipulates each area.' I like to stick to the Alexander term 'inhibit', though I often also use the phrase 'Say NO to reacting', rather than allowing pupils to think in terms familiar to them like 'I must relax' or 'prevent' a reaction, though terms like 'Let go', 'Don't hang on' or 'Think of releasing but don't do it' often help. A good teacher has to be quite devious sometimes to bring about certain improvements and has to try all sorts of approaches.

Different words can mean different things to different people. All the more reason to stick to Alexander's terms and get the pupil on to this new wavelength, probably thinking in terms that are at this stage strange and unfamiliar.

There are no set rules regarding teaching methods, short of teaching the basic principles, and all teachers will vary somewhat in their approach as in any subject. F.M. often allowed his assistants to take over with the lying-down work after he had brought about miraculous changes to pupils working on them in chairs or standing. However, for we more ordinary mortals, and with the improvement over the years in teaching methods, lying down is usually an important part of the Alexander lesson.

In the early lessons I like to work on a couch regularly, as I find that pupils can take in what is being said to them more easily than if they are moving around or trying to maintain a better upright state. The danger here is that pupils do not think of their lessons as times for working, but mainly as sessions in which they will release a lot of tension and come out feeling better. It cannot be emphasised too often that what is needed by most pupils is a great deal of work to bring about, maintain and gain more improvement. It is fairly easy to take away a pupil's tensions but much more difficult to put something better in its place in the way of more stability, improved muscle tone, a better balance and alignment with the maximum of freedom and changed centre of gravity and all the various elements that make up an improved manner of use. For certain types of people, releasing too much unnecessary tension too quickly can be very frightening and disorientating, as they will have been relying a great deal on those tension patterns in many areas of their lives and will possibly not return for the next lesson. A good teacher will assess carefully how fast each individual pupil can progress. For myself, I find that working on a couch in the early lessons can bring about speedier progress and better experiences for the pupil than only working in an upright position, sitting or standing. There is a danger, though, that the pupil will simply fall asleep. So many people are dead-tired but do not know this until they have let go of some of the tension that has been disguising their true state. An experienced teacher will pick this up immediately and probably change the emphasis in the lesson.

It helps pupils in the very early lessons if they are acquainted with F.M.'s story as they then realise the sort of journey they themselves are about to embark upon, and the parallels and similarities between their own and Alexander's experiences, and why we work in the way that he had to. Most pupils are in fact interested in how the Technique evolved and who Alexander was. (I myself thought for some time that the Technique was called after the psycho-therapist Dr Franz Alexander and knew nothing about F.M. until I read about him.)

With most of us the stimulus/response mechanism is locked together so firmly that we go around like automata, with no thought or control over our actions. We need to learn to make a gap between the stimulus and the response to it, so that we can then use our brains and begin to think about how we react. Alexander said that the most important side of his work was as an exercise in finding out what thinking is. We often think we are thinking, but are merely reacting or feeling.

So inhibition cannot be over-emphasised in these early lessons as most people's reactions are firmly established: frequently reflex or instantaneous. Their habits are deeply seated and of long standing and all their feelings are related to them. If we are to learn to control these areas of our lives we probably need to start at a fairly simple level. Even in apparently quite trivial activities like sitting and standing, walking, talking, combing the hair, turning a tap, filling a kettle and so on, the sort of acts we perform quite unconsciously, we are all tending to reinforce old habits of use and bring into play old familiar patterns. Frequently these are harmful, to some extent, and often can be grossly so. Pupils should be encouraged from the outset to notice just how they rush into old familiar ways of reacting without thinking, and, although they can probably do little about it at this stage, at least they can become aware of the dangers of continuing in this way.

This necessary new control over strong habitual responses and old habits is quite difficult for most pupils so it is important at the outset not to make matters too hard and to keep the stimuli fairly simple or apparently trivial; though when a pupil latches on to this idea he can bring about a whole world of change and improvement through refusing immediate consent to the old response. A whole lifetime's poor experience is at that moment being discarded and we are looking at the situation unblinkered by old ideas and unfettered by old habits, freeing ourselves for the possibility of real change in our lives.

The changing process can be very alarming. It is after all a

There are countless examples of misuse everywhere we go

voyage into the unknown, but one cannot hope to bring about change which is essentially unfamiliar by perpetuating and reinforcing familiar habits; so the unfamiliar result – improvement through change – necessitates an unfamiliar means – Inhibition and Ordering. Most pupils, if they are properly motivated in wanting to do something about themselves, will accept this rather frightening prospect, as most of them will come to realise that the unknown can be better than the known which they are not happy with, providing they can understand and control the means of change. The skilful teacher will make the transition as pleasant and unalarming as possible.

Unlike many of the newer techniques around, the Alexander Technique does not claim to change you overnight, and is essentially gentle, natural and geared to the individual's capacities and needs. This does not make it any easier but it does guarantee that the change is real change and not some spurious lurch forward in one's progress through life that seems better but is in fact only temporary. As the real work has to be done mainly by the pupil after a time, though usually guided by a teacher, it is always under the pupil's control and can be carefully monitored.

Having clearly established the principle of Inhibition the pupil should then be introduced to Alexander's idea of the Primary Control, the sorting out of the neck/head/back relationship, and to the various elements involved in the idea of Ordering or Directing.

Despite gross misuse, some performers such as the late John Ogden are still brilliant; but improved body use could only benefit their functioning and well-being

Direction

The first area of the body that most of us tend to interfere with unnecessarily is the neck. Often we over-involve the neck muscles and thereby lose the free poise and delicate balance of the head.

The first Primary Order: 'Neck release'

In the development, growth and functioning of most vertebrates the head is designed to lead or initiate a reaction or movement. If it is interfered with, it cannot do this, and harmful compensations tend to occur lower down in the structure. That is, if the head does not lead, the rest cannot follow properly, so, conversely: allow the head to lead and the rest will tend to follow more reasonably. However, most of us prevent the head playing its 'leading role' by pulling the neck muscles out of balance and over-involving them. This usually involves the big, outer muscles of the neck which exert traction on the head, i.e., they pull it back, forwards, sideways or downwards. This prevents the tiny inner muscles around the top two vertebrae playing their proper role in conjunction with these vertebrae: that of allowing the head to be correctly balanced and freely poised on the top of the spine. So there is an imbalance between the inner and outer muscles, and often an imbalance in the outer muscles themselves.

Occasionally one will find a neck that is almost too free, whose muscles are flaccid and do not support the heavy head in a light and balanced way. This then becomes a problem of encouraging tone, by getting the neck to connect up with the back and the rest of the spine, and coaxing the dynamic lightness that the 'leading head' should have. The neck muscles are rather like the guy ropes around a flag pole. If one is too tight it pulls the pole over, but if one is too loose the pole also topples over. But usually the case is one of a stiffened neck where the muscles are over-worked in some way. This naturally affects the bony structure, the cervical spine, and can pull it out of its natural alignment. Frequently this is a dropped forward curve to the spine, poking forward from an area between the shoulder-blades, usually slightly above them, a very important and delicate area in the nervous system, creating a 'hump'. This is very common and is clearly seen in the adolescent slump and in those adopting a hang-dog expression, the punk-type stance or fashionable 'laid-back' attitude.

A pleasing neck/head
relationship

The neck can be over-straightened with the natural curve
ironed out too much – as seen sometimes in ballet dancers who
have forced their necks to lengthen but who hold them just as
stiffly as those which are shortened and pulled down into the
shoulders, or the 'bull neck' with which most of us are familiar.
Obviously these variations need different approaches, though
both will require the neck muscles to release before any improvement can take place, as will pulling the neck over to the side,
twisting it, or any of the other many ways of interfering with it. A
good teacher will recognise these variations whether they are
gross or subtle, occurring all of the time or just some of the time,
perhaps happening only in particular movements, activities, or
reactions, or maybe permanently distorted with tension, and will
approach the problem appropriately. But as most of us, much of
the time, are stiffening our necks in some way or other, the first
Primary Order or Direction is 'Neck release' or 'Neck to be free".
This order must be given or projected but NOT DONE. At this
stage it is a purely verbal order reminding the pupil to direct
attention to the neck without trying to do anything to release it.

The unbalanced use of the neck muscles, as we have seen, creates an interference with the free poise and balance of the head. This is usually at the base of the skull where the spine goes up into it and where it pivots – the sub-occipital joint – as though pulling back the whole mass of the head to meet some point between the shoulder-blades. Again, some people do this grossly all the time, others more subtly or just some of the time, perhaps within certain movements or for certain activities; and whilst we might also interfere with the poise and balance of the head in other ways as well, perhaps pulling it to the side or twisting it round, nearly everyone seems to pull it back and down to some extent. There are many ways of interfering with the balancing mechanism of a freely poised head but pulling it back and down is almost universal, hence the order 'Head forward and up'.

Do not try to 'position' the head correctly – the very word suggests something fixed. The head should be free – dynamically so – the controlled leading mechanism, not just flopping around.

Do not try to 'do' these orders. If you try to 'put' the head forward, almost at once it goes forward and *down*. So it must be *thought* forward in relation to the top of the spine so as to prevent any tightening at the base of the skull, or any tendency to fix it there, or pull it back.

If the neck has already dropped too far forward from the 'hump', any tendency to over-'forward' the head will emphasise this, but as such a situation usually encourages one to pull the

The second Primary Order: 'Head forward and up'

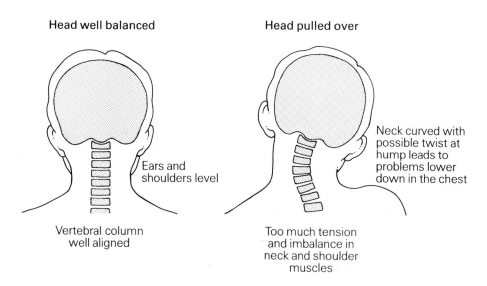

Head well balanced

Head pulled over

Ears and shoulders level

Vertebral column well aligned

Neck curved with possible twist at hump leads to problems lower down in the chest

Too much tension and imbalance in neck and shoulder muscles

head back simply to look ahead or speak, merely NOT pulling the head back can feel very odd, it might even 'feel' forward and DOWN but in relation to the spine it is not.

If you try to 'put' the head up it is often confused with pulling the chin up, which could mean that the mass of the head is pulled back, or the whole head is forced upwards, leading to an even more stiffened and perhaps an over-straightened neck. It should be neither over-'forwarded' nor over-'upped'.

'Forward' does not mean the whole face poking forward (as this would surely take the neck forward), nor chin jutting forward (as this usually means the head is pulled back), though sometimes the jaw will need to release forward but this is separate from the main part of the skull. The neck and head have to be re-educated together as the one affects the other; but the orders are self-checking in that if you over-do the 'forward' the head goes forward and DOWN and if you over-do the UP it can go back and down again. We mostly need both directions and *in the right sequence*: the head cannot go up off the top of the spine if it is at all jammed or pulled back. Strictly speaking the head simply needs to be left alone to play the role it is designed to play, but this means very little to most people, as they have very little experience of leaving it alone, the idea has to be emphasised constantly, so forgive me if I seem to labour the point.

As the centre of gravity of the head is in front of the top of the spine, the pivoting point, if there were no muscles involved it would drop forward and down, but, as there are strong muscles often over-involved, most commonly it tends to be pulled back

Head back and down

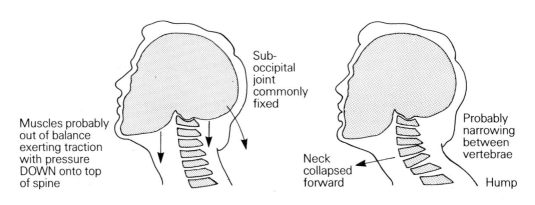

Muscles probably out of balance exerting traction with pressure DOWN onto top of spine

Sub-occipital joint commonly fixed

Neck collapsed forward

Probably narrowing between vertebrae

Hump

and down. So we need a happy balance and sorting out of three things: pivot, centre of gravity, and use of muscles.

If the tone in the neck muscles is good and well-balanced these elements tend to get sorted out. But there are many complicated ways of distorting the neck-and-head relationship and the skilled teacher should be able to alert the pupil to the many possibilities of going awry and to wrong conceptions.

Again I must emphasise NOT TO TRY TO DO these orders. Do not try to free the neck or put the head forward and up. Wiggling the head about or exercising the neck by rotating the head does not usually do much good as most people would merely rotate the head by exercising the habitual patterns in the neck muscles, patterns which they are trying to change. It has to happen through UNdoing and you cannot DO an UNdoing, you can only STOP doing something which will allow the undoing to take place. Most of us in the early stages of the lessons do not really know what a free neck and a freely poised head are anyway. If we have them, it is more than likely to be a mere accident: perhaps we have had a particularly good night's sleep, or are on holiday or have something nice to look forward to. But the free neck and freely poised head have nothing to do with any conscious control and knowledge of what the better state should be. Now we can begin to get back to this better state through a more consciously controlled means, and awareness of how we interfere and lose it. Maybe we will lose it less readily and perhaps get back to it more often, so that we can begin to appreciate a more reasonable 'norm', where the neck muscles are in a good state of balance and the head

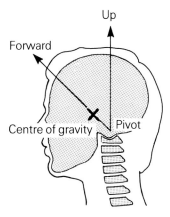

Head well balanced, forward and up

Up

Forward

Centre of gravity

Pivot

Neck well aligned, muscles in balance

Head forward and down

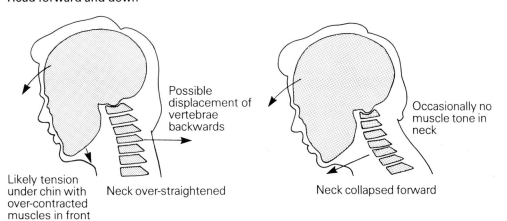

Possible displacement of vertebrae backwards

Neck over-straightened

Likely tension under chin with over-contracted muscles in front of neck

Occasionally no muscle tone in neck

Neck collapsed forward

41

becomes once again the dynamically leading mechanism and balancing agent in the way the body works.

'Head forward and up' will, however, change its meaning as the neck and head relationship changes and improves, and depends on what the subject is doing at any given moment or his or her state at that time. It is NOT a position for the head but a direction. It simply means a lack of anything that is interfering with the free poise and balance of the head, which most commonly is pulling it back and down, hence 'forward and up'.

The third Primary Order: 'Back lengthen and widen'

Mis-use of the back

If the head is frequently interfered with, this will adversely affect the back by creating a certain amount of pressure *down* the spine as though each vertebra were pressing down on to the next one.

- Standing with the knees braced back as when supposedly standing up 'straight'.
- Pulling the knees together through a shortening of the inner part of the thigh, which often accompanies the common practice of crossing the knees when seated.
- Sticking out the bottom when sitting down.
- Collapsing in the lower back when seated.
- Standing with one leg braced and the other bent and the pelvis displaced sideways like Michelangelo's David.

All these sorts of mis-use in the lower parts of the body will tend to create pressure up the spine, so with what is going wrong at the top end and with what is going wrong at the bottom, it is almost as though the spine is being pressed from either end, resulting in a shortening and often in excessive curves. These displacements are common in the lower back, the lumbar area, causing a sway back (lordosis) and a displacement of the pelvis, tipping it forward and taking with it all the major organs in that area, creating too much pressure over the balls of the feet. Sometimes the problem is a little higher up in the middle back just below the shoulder-blades. Often allied to a very held chest and a raised breast-bone (sternum), it is common in classically trained dancers and is

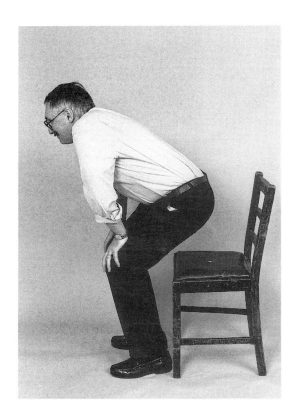

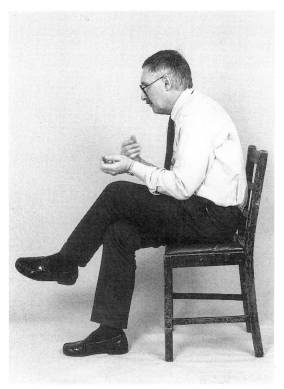

frequently caused by a wrong idea of 'standing up straight' with the 'chest out and shoulders back' as one is frequently exhorted to do as a child. The result is faulty breathing and is often linked to strong emotional states of fear, aggression or anxiety.

It is not uncommon to find both the lower and middle back concave states together. The 'hump' (kyphosis) – curve or drop from the area between the shoulder-blades – is also common as I've already pointed out. The 'hump' can be disguised if the lower back is very concave and, until this is sorted out, is sometimes not apparent. Sometimes it can be a sideways curve of the spine, lower or middle back, sometimes both (scoliosis), often allied to a twist in the chest. Maybe there will be no excessive curves, merely a crunching down of each vertebra on to the next with no tone in the muscles supporting the vertebral column, or muscles that are permanently over-contracted in this area, resulting in a straight but very fixed and shortened lower back. It is also possible to have an over-straightened lower back which is not

43

This is a typical way of standing, with most things awry. Even Michelangelo's David was not immune

shortened: this, like the over-straightened neck, can be a very difficult problem and generally has to be dealt with through encouraging lots of muscular release in this area. It is another common problem in ballet dancers through 'tucking under' the pelvis. Occasionally the problem is very subtle, perhaps just a couple of vertebrae out of alignment but resulting in a lack of connection in that part of the spine which will not be able to take its fair share of the work-load, the discs in that area perhaps not playing their proper cushioning role, and in turn another area of the spine will become overworked, perhaps a little lower down the back, and will thereby become another vulnerable area.

These are just a few of the many ways of mis-using the back which will cause problems often leading to pain. When assessing the state of the back the teacher will not only take into account such things but also the amount of tension there is in the buttocks, the natural size of the bottom and the pupil's basic physical type.

So now, after the neck and the head, we need to attend to the back, ordering it first to 'lengthen'. You can, however, over-lengthen the spine, creating a rigidly straight back which I have already pointed out is common in certain dancers, or perhaps those grand ladies over-concerned with 'posture'. The spine should be *flexibly* lengthening with slight natural curves, not excessive curves. When lying down it should be able to mould itself easily to the surface in a lengthened state and not be held up off the couch, floor or mattress, but nor should it be rigidly flattened with excessive pressure downwards. If the spine is over-lengthened this will also result in a narrowing of the back and an interference with the free movement of the rib cage sideways for natural breathing, and a displacement of the shoulders on top of the thorax. So the back also needs to 'widen' so that the structure is free for good breathing, with the necessary tone and support and the shoulders comfortably placed on the thorax and integrated in with the back. However, the widening can also be over-done: you see boxers, wrestlers, body-builders, even certain singers with over-broadened backs, resulting in a shortening of the spine to achieve this excessive widening. Of course some people will be naturally wider or longer than others so their basic physical type must always be borne in mind.

A balance of length and width is desirable and so the order is 'Back lengthen and widen'. It is self-checking – over-lengthen and

'Chin up, shoulders back, chest out' is not a good way to stand!

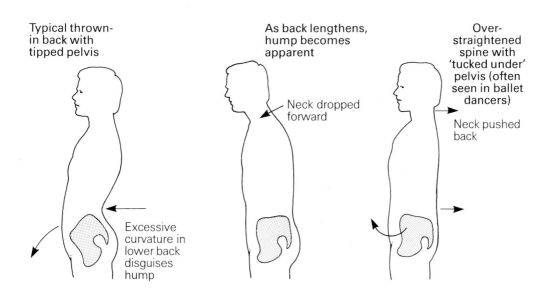

Typical thrown-in back with tipped pelvis

Excessive curvature in lower back disguises hump

As back lengthens, hump becomes apparent

Neck dropped forward

Over-straightened spine with 'tucked under' pelvis (often seen in ballet dancers)

Neck pushed back

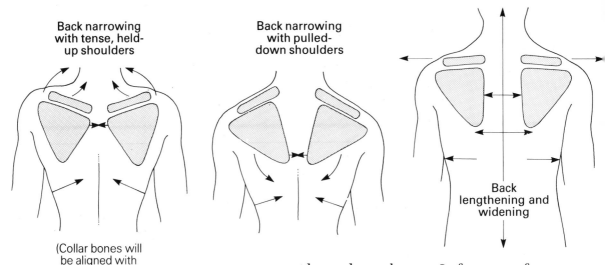

Back narrowing with tense, held-up shoulders

Back narrowing with pulled-down shoulders

Back lengthening and widening

(Collar bones will be aligned with top edge of shoulder blades)

you narrow; over-widen and you shorten. In fact most of us are shortening and narrowing at the same time and so need more of both elements. Strictly speaking, the order should be '*Spine* lengthen and back widen' but it makes for a simpler verbal formula to say '*Back* lengthen and widen'. Even the simplest movement or reaction involves the brain, nervous system, muscles, tendons, ligaments, joints and so on. Obviously we cannot attend to all these things each time we wish to act or we would never get anything done, so the simpler the formula to cover all these areas the more effective it will be.

The back should not be thought to end at the base of the neck but, as it is governed largely by the working of the spine, to go right up into the skull. So in a sense the neck is considered twice whilst the other parts are considered once, firstly with the 'neck release' order, then again with the 'back lengthen' order, but, as the neck is the key to everything coming undone and then being put back together again properly, it is no bad thing to give it this extra emphasis. There are other good physiological reasons for extra attention being paid to the neck which I will discuss later.

We now have three areas to attend to: the neck, which affects the head, which affects the back. It is important to keep to the right sequence of orders. You cannot easily have a lengthening and widening back if you are constantly interfering with the free poise and balance of the head, and you certainly cannot have this poise and balance if you are constantly stiffening the neck, so it has to be neck, head and back in that order. You are *letting* the neck release, to *let* the head go forward and up, to *let* the back lengthen and widen.

It is important for the pupil to have these Primary Orders firmly established at this stage. Not repeating the words parrot-fashion but attending to the areas to which you are directing the orders so that you are becoming more aware of what is going on in these areas and bringing more conscious control to bear over them. I think it is important to use the same words that Alexander worked out so that we are all speaking the same language with the same terminology. Much of the confusion and apparent nonsense being talked and written about the Alexander Technique is, I suspect, because people prefer their own terms, or use words associated with other disciplines and add to the muddle by thinking they know better than the technique's originator. If the terms are properly explained by the teacher they are a way of keeping the work simple, pure and free of unnecessary mystery.

One of Alexander's many strokes of genius must be to have devised a formula that covers most eventualities and needs. Most of us often need to release our necks, gain free poise and balance to the head by allowing it to go forward and up, and thereby gain the needed greater length and width in the back. It is as near as we can get in words to what most of us need much of the time. Whilst one or other elements might be needed more by one person than by another and more emphasis might in time be placed on this particular element, each one depends upon the others and all three need to be considered in the correct sequence; you can only free the neck so far but then when you get the back working you can often free it some more. To gain more improvement and keep it we have constantly to return to this hierarchy of attention.

These orders or directions are at this stage largely *preventive orders*, checking that at least matters are not made worse. As you order your neck to release, you should at the very least not do anything more to stiffen it. As you order the head to go forward and up, you should not do anything more in the way of pulling it back and down. And as you order the back to lengthen and widen, you should not do anything more to shorten or narrow it. If we can stop the slide down the slippery slope of mis-use, we can then begin the journey of change and improved use and more efficient functioning. These preventive orders being projected, the next reaction or movement cannot make things worse, and might well be considerably better, even if at this stage it does not feel better.

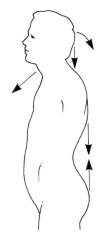

Back shortened with neck poked forward, head and back down, excessive lower back curve and flaccid abdominal muscles

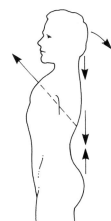

Back shortened with neck stiffened, head back and down. Raised breast bone leads to middle back problems. Lumbar curve probable

Back lengthening from base to top of spine

Linking Primary Orders to experiences

Although at the outset these orders are essentially preventive, and should continue to be so, as the pupil progresses he should begin to link the orders to certain experiences he should have in his lessons: experiences of releasing tension, gaining tone, changing the work-load in the body and the balance and centre of gravity, greater freedom in the joints, more stability, channelling the energy more reasonably, in fact all the things that go towards an improved manner of use. Strictly speaking, I suppose, it does not really matter what the form of words is that we use and link on to these new improved experiences; but as we are supposed to be intelligent beings we might as well get as near as we can in the form of words to what is required. The words, in time, recall and trigger off the better experience, so the simpler we keep them the better and more effective our response will be, with as little confusion as possible to our poor bewildered minds. Pupils will frequently complicate matters if they possibly can, so it is best to limit the opportunities for so doing.

As the teacher takes the pupil's head, for example, the words 'Neck release; head forward and up' should be projected and linked on to the coaxing of greater freedom in the neck muscles and the improvement in the balance of the head. Or as the teacher manipulates the back, encouraging the pupil to stop tightening, shortening or narrowing it, so the back orders begin to mean more and more. And so the positive side to the ordering process is being built up gradually as the pupil progresses, alongside the preventive aspect which will continue to be important as the tendency to revert to old patterns will be very strong at least to begin with, and will stay with many of us for a long time.

The preventive side of ordering is fairly easy to understand from the start but the more positive side is not so, as the experiences associated with it have not yet been consciously experienced; it should be built up slowly at the pace appropriate to the pupil's ability to absorb change. A skilled teacher should pace matters suitably and not try to get results before the pupil is ready. As I've explained, the teacher might need to work more on one aspect of the neck/head/back relationship than on the others, depending on the pupil's deficiencies, but as each is dependent on the others, at this stage all three have to be attended to in the right sequence.

Eventually the orders should encompass a whole world of meaning to us, not only in the lessons but away from them: in the preventive sense of not going back into old bad habits but also preventing the build-up of new bad habits. These orders also allow us to monitor what state we are in, and what we are doing to ourselves at any given moment, not just in the realm of stiffening the neck, interfering with the head and back, but checking whether we are twisted, off-balance, over-involving the shoulders, collapsing, fixing, bracing, stiffening, hunching, and perhaps, most importantly, allowing us to attend to the next reaction or movement so that it can be more appropriate and reasonable.

Many pupils are remarkably reluctant to attend to themselves in this way. It is not surprising, I suppose, when we are encouraged from an early age to DO something about ourselves: do it properly, concentrate, work hard, stand up straight, and so on, all of which involves effort, often strain and wear and tear on the structure, and frequently it is just such effort that has got us into the mess we are trying to get out of. We are trying to bring about something better by doing all the old things, but even more strongly, and then we wonder why things only get worse. Concentration often implies effort. How often are children regarded by teachers suspiciously if they appear to be at ease and not trying hard? The furrowed brow and hunched shoulders are deemed to be desirable as they are signs of hard work being done, whereas in fact they are probably preventing the child giving his full attention to the matter in hand as they are creating a barrier of tension between the subject and the object of his attention. The quality of attention should be light and gentle but regular. For this reason I do not like my pupils to close their eyes when they are lying down on the couch even though they think they can 'concentrate' better that way. Sometimes, of course, they are very tired and cannot help it but then the rest in itself will do them good, or perhaps they have a large amount of facial tension in which case it might be temporarily permissible. However, if they get used to projecting the orders with the eyes closed it can become an internalising process, possibly valuable in calming the pupil in a similar way to meditation, but they can hypnotise themselves slightly this way and it becomes something they only associate with 'relaxing'. Ideally it should be much more than that, a way of making us aware of ourselves in relation to our environment on all sorts of

The quality of attention

It is a common misconception that strain and misuse must accompany good concentration

levels, and by closing the eyes we immediately cut out a major area of awareness.

If we get used to giving the orders to ourselves whilst taking in what is going on around us the progress might at first seem slower, but in time it is better progress allied to a fuller, deeper and broader awareness, and it all becomes easier with practice. We *can* think about many things at once in spite of our school teachers' exhortations to do the opposite. It is strange that conventional education, which is supposed to be helping us to use our brain, is often constraining us in this area. We are not taught how to think.

Pupils sometimes seem a little embarrassed when asked to attend to themselves in this fashion, especially the apparently more 'intelligent' types who are used to a high degree of achievement and getting good results. The simpler, in the best sense of the word, type of person often tends to be able to give a better quality of attention to himself through not complicating matters unnecessarily. It is often useful to suggest at this point that you do not expect the pupil to believe a word you say as a teacher but you do expect them to listen carefully to what you suggest, try it, and they will find out for themselves.

Most of us want to cheat a little and expedite the improvement by 'doing' something, but this 'end-gaining' attitude never helps in the long run. Little do we realise, at this stage, how strong a force in our lives these inner patterns that need attention can be, and how they need sorting out just as much as the outer physical patterns. It is sometimes useful to point out that even at the most basic level of all when you 'order' something to release you might at that moment STOP DOING something which is preventing the release. If you fix an electrode to a part of the body and just think of moving it but do not actually do it, that thought will register on an electromyograph which measures muscle tension. Also, by ordering, one can calm down the brain as well as the body, gaining a less excitable state akin to and associated with the production of Alpha Rhythms in the brain and perhaps the lowering of blood pressure.

If you stop doing something, then muscles will obviously release to some extent, depending on what sort of use they have been subjected to. There is, however, an extra element of releasing and lengthening which can be achieved purely by ordering.

I hope that I have made it clear that the ordering process contains many elements and goes on at several levels at once. Ideally the teacher should encourage the pupil to be content merely giving his orders at this stage rather than worrying about improvement or achieving anything; only then will he be on his way to being able to accomplish things in a better way. He should be happier attending to the 'means' rather than the 'ends', whereupon he will start to find that he is actually getting better results through this new unfamiliar attention to 'means whereby'.

By projecting these orders we are working directly on the nervous system. As the pupil is manipulated by the teacher so we are working on the musculature which affects the bony structure and alignment of the body which affects the working of the major organs and circulation, a change of balance and centre of gravity; and so a great deal should be happening from the outset in these lessons. As they progress, secondary or subsidiary orders can be added, but at the start it is more than enough and quite fundamentally important to attend through the Main Orders to the primarily controlling area of the body.

Working method

Having firmly established the method of working and progressing through the two basic principles of Inhibition and Direction or Ordering, the third vital element in the teaching of the technique – that of Working on Oneself – should be introduced as and when it is thought appropriate. There is little that pupils can do about themselves at first and they are bound to lapse into old bad habits between early sessions, but if the lessons are sufficiently close together this will happen less and less and they will begin to maintain the improvement so that the lessons can be spaced further apart. It makes things easier for both pupil and teacher to have the first ten or a dozen lessons as near together as possible, ideally at least three a week for the first three or four weeks then spacing them out a little more. In the earlier days of teaching pupils were expected to attend every day for two or three weeks at least, and it is still not a bad idea, but it is often not possible for reasons of time and money, and with the improvement in teaching methods it is not quite so important. Pupils *can* make enormous progress with one lesson a week but this depends on a strong motivation and on getting the pupil to work on himself quite early on, not easy for most of us, but various ways of working on oneself should be introduced during the course of the lessons and ways of applying the technique should be suggested.

I will return to this aspect of the Technique frequently later on as I consider it to be enormously important and often neglected by many teachers, who tend to tell their pupils not to worry about it. Whilst they cannot do a great deal at the outset, and to work in the wrong way would be counter-productive, unless you want the pupil to keep returning for lessons for the rest of his life or till he gets bored and you are merely manipulating and not teaching the pupil, then this aspect cannot be neglected, and if so it indicates a poor or inarticulate teacher or a lazy pupil. It is the most frequent complaint that one hears from pupils, that they do not know how to 'keep it going'.

I would now like to describe in some detail what happens when the pupil is being worked on.

The lying down position

The pupil will start by sitting up on the couch with feet towards one end, either with knees bent or legs straight out whichever is the more comfortable, but not pulling the knees together, and preferably with the feet spaced slightly further apart than the width of the pelvis, and with the bottom positioned so that he or she does not overshoot the end of the couch when lying down. After inhibiting the idea or suggestion to lie down, and thereby not immediately flopping down in some old, familiar way, the pupil should then project the three main guiding orders so that some thought is being given as to 'how' the movement will take place, in fact using it to bring about a slightly better state. Whilst the pupil might well be stiffening his or her neck, interfering with the balance of the head and with the working of the back, not to mention other problems like hunched shoulders or a held breast-bone, at least things cannot get worse if the pupil is attending to him or herself properly; in fact some considerable improvement in the way of releasing tension and gaining more fullness in the back can happen within the movement. It is often a good idea to think of going UP when going back or down as it tends to prevent collapsing or a contraction downwards, but it is interesting to notice how many pupils actually *look* up or raise themselves in some way when you just suggest they *think* up and so once again they reinforce some old idea and are not properly inhibiting, or thinking.

Having given the right kind of preparatory attention through Inhibition and Ordering, the pupil will then allow the movement to take place, and with the teacher's hands guiding and directing will lie down whilst maintaining the inhibition of the old stimulus and the neck/head/back direction. It is often a good idea to breathe out whilst moving, as it is less easy to fix than when breathing in and prevents holding the breath. This attention to the 'means whereby', how he or she carried out the movement, should allow for some improvement within the action. There should be less habitual stiffening of the neck, the head should be allowed, as it were, to 'lead" the movement: the back should be used in a more lengthened way in conjunction with an appropriate amount of tone in the abdominal muscles, though it is usually a good idea to think of letting the tummy go so that no unnecessary tightening goes on here. As the pupil reaches the lying-down

Think 'up' even when lying down, allowing the head to lead throughout the movement

position the head will be placed on a number of supporting books or on a small cushion or pad. The height of this will depend on several factors: the degree of tension in the neck, the natural curve of the cervical spine, the shape of the skull and the muscularity of the shoulders. A good teacher will immediately know the amount of support suitable for the individual's needs, depending on the above factors as well as his or her state at that particular time and on the general changing process. The individual's state at any given moment is not easy to determine subjectively at first, so once again the help of the teacher is important, though gradually as the lessons progress they become more aware and in tune with their real state. Often, as improvement occurs over a period, less support is needed under the head, as the neck, when freer, will often drop down slightly to the couch.

Certain books on the technique and others that suggest the Alexander lying-down position as a way of 'relaxing' – perhaps as applied to voice production – do not indicate the precise amount of support needed under the head. In fact often they do not suggest any at all, which would more than likely allow the pupil to continue to be pulling back the head at the base of the skull just to rest the head on the floor, and thereby cause a certain amount of pressure down the spine as well. As one of the reasons for lying down like this is to gain some length in the spine, if there is no support for the head it is as though there are two opposing forces at work here. The amount of support can vary from none at all, very rare, to as much as six inches (fifteen centimetres) with extremely kyphotic, or hunched, types, but on average would be between one and two inches (two and half to five centimetres). The expert help of a teacher is obviously useful here with this basic but important point which can easily be overlooked. Sometimes, with the required support under the head, the pupil can feel rather constricted in the throat area, but this problem gradually disappears as the relationships of the various parts in this area become sorted out. It is better to put up with this for a while than continue with the worst habit in this region, that of pulling back the head in relation to the neck, as this tends to set up a whole chain-reaction of harmful pressures throughout the structure.

Having lain down, the pupil will be asked to direct his attention again to himself, and frequently little pockets of tension can be discovered by checking various areas. Maybe he *did* stiffen the neck during the lying-down movement and so, with the teacher's help, this can then be eased. Just thinking of the back of the neck dropping down towards the surface of the couch – providing the pupil does not push the head back into the supporting books – can bring about a certain amount of releasing. The same will possibly be true in various areas which the teacher will take note of and deal with in the correct sequence. So, with the pupil having let go as much as possible without forcing anything to change or be rearranged, but merely thinking and attending, the teacher will

Lying down – bad

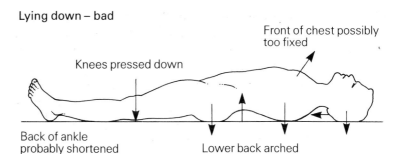

Front of chest possibly too fixed

Knees pressed down

Back of ankle probably shortened

Lower back arched

Lying down – good

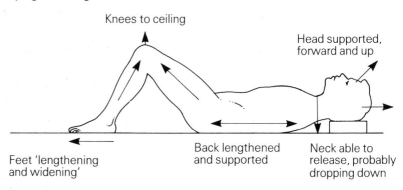

Knees to ceiling

Head supported, forward and up

Feet 'lengthening and widening'

Back lengthened and supported

Neck able to release, probably dropping down

then begin, with the pupil's consent, to deal with the various problems through gentle manipulation. This should be a joint affair, it is no good the teacher trying to bring about an improvement in the realignment and relationing of one area to another if the pupil is resisting. Nor should the pupil help, as he or she is then likely to have preconceived ideas of what is required, and so possibly bring into play old familiar muscle patterns, many of which will need to be changed. As the teacher begins to adjust a particular area, the pupil will again need to inhibit the teacher's hands, refusing to react by helping or hindering. The pupil will then attend to the guiding orders in sequence, so that he or she is leaving him- or herself alone, as well as perhaps giving a little extra attention to the area being dealt with, but always in relation to this main sequence, which helps to maintain an awareness of the total pattern of the body. The process should generally be slow as the pupil has a great deal to attend to, and at first will not be able to spread his or her attention easily into several areas. The pupil must be given lots of time to return frequently to the three main guiding orders.

When lying down some teachers prefer their pupils to project the order 'Head forward and *out*' rather than 'forward and *up*' as it seems to make more sense when in a lying-down position. This, however, means that they have one order for lying down and another for when they are in an upright state, and only complicates things. In any case it does not matter where you are in space – lying, standing, sitting or at an angle – it is the relationship of head to neck which is important; 'forward' simply means do not pull the head *back* and 'up' means 'do not pull it *down* on the top of the spine'.

When you lie down it is a good idea to notice how the arms fall. They should be slightly bent with the elbows away from the side of the body and the hands down towards the couch. Alternatively, place them on the chest, the tummy or the hip-bones. The elbows should not be in towards the side of the trunk with the hands upwards as is suggested in certain books, as this indicates a mis-use of the arms and shoulders, a twist in the shoulder joint and often an over-contraction of the inner part of the upper arms (biceps). When the shoulders become free the arms will naturally fall in this way, and there is no harm in encouraging them to do so from the outset.

At this point the teacher might want to move the pupil's legs, first one and then the other, so that they are flexed at the hip, the knees raised pointing upwards towards the ceiling with the order: 'Knees to the ceiling', the feet flat on the couch, slightly wider apart than the width of the pelvis and slightly turned out in line with the rest of the leg. The angle of the thigh, lower part of the leg and the surface of the couch will then be forming something like an equilateral triangle.

Once again the idea of the leg being moved must be inhibited and the main attention to the neck, head and back maintained as the movement is allowed to take place; it is just a question of letting the knee bend without the pupil taking over, resisting or helping, which is quite difficult, especially when there are strong reflex patterns in the legs, particularly those of athletic types and dancers, with the tendons at the back of the knee frequently tightening overmuch. With both legs in this new place it is common for pupils to want to pull the knees together too much, or in the more athletic types to brace them apart. It is sometimes a good idea to suggest that the pupil think of the knees being attached by strings to the ceiling, but this comes into the realm of

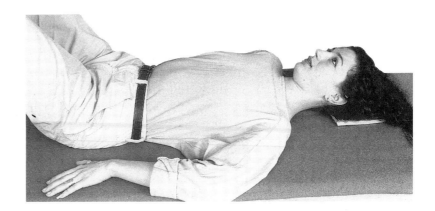

The hands should be placed like this

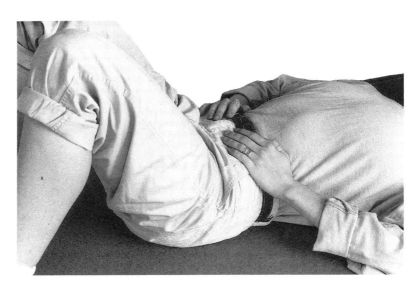

. . . or like this

Secondary Orders and what 'leaving things alone' feels like which I shall enlarge upon later. With the legs in this new place a better balance of the antagonistic muscles can be brought about, with less pressure into the hip joints, and it is a better way of encouraging this balance in the leg muscles than if the legs were left straight out along the couch. Also it often encourages a release in the usually tightened lower back muscles. You cannot hope to establish good tone without first encouraging good balance through releasing.

The back

Whilst constantly returning to check the neck-and-head relationship to see that the pupil is not interfering with it unnecessarily or to coax even more improvement in this area, the teacher might then begin to consider sorting out the back. He will probably put his hands under the back from the top end, going under the shoulders, sliding down the couch with his hands downwards so as not to disturb the pupil unduly, who should in turn be once again inhibiting the stimulus of these hands, that is, not accommodating them in any way by helping the teacher to reach under his back, perhaps raising the front of the chest or the shoulders, nor hindering by pressing down and making it difficult for the

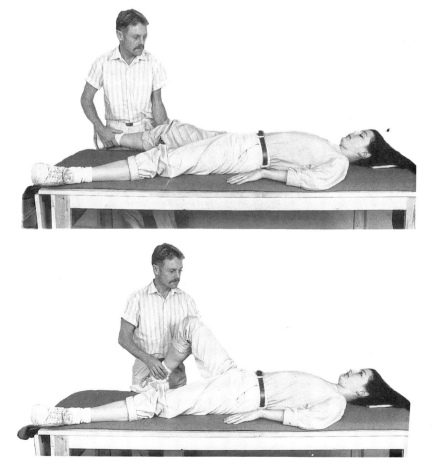

Taking the leg 'out', flexing at the hip, and placing it in the raised, well-balanced, position

59

teacher. The teacher will then turn his or her hands upwards, checking the pupil's back, and as the pupil projects the order 'Back lengthen and widen', associating it with what the teacher is now doing, will then manipulate the back with a 'scooping' motion, encouraging it to lengthen and widen so that perhaps it will drop down more, spreading over the couch. But a good teacher will also be releasing other patterns that might be encouraging a twist of the rib cage or more shortening on one side of the trunk than on the other. As there are many ways of mis-using the back so there are many areas for the teacher to deal with in this single undoing movement. This is often very pleasant and a great relief to a pupil who has been creating a lot of tension in the back, as the couch will then be supporting the back in a fuller and better way, taking over much of the work and effort that the pupil had been making by hanging on to the back muscles, shortening them and pulling them out of balance.

The lower back and pelvic area will also probably need attention and the teacher can attack this by placing the hands under the pupil's buttocks, with the pupil's knees either together or still apart, and adjusting the pelvis by encouraging still more length in the lower back area, allowing it to settle down on the couch even more. Again there might well be twists and other asymmetrical patterns in the pelvis to sort out, as well as tension in the buttocks. With very fat people and those with very fixed lower backs this manoeuvre can be quite difficult and might not seem to be effective for some time, perhaps only when other areas of the body have become freer. During all this the pupil should still, of course, be attending to leaving the neck and head alone and linking the 'Back lengthen' idea on to this coaxing of extra length in the lumbar area, rather like a two-way stretch.

If there are twists in the rib cage or pelvis to be sorted out the pupil will no doubt have become familiar with these habitual patterns: being untwisted may well feel odd or even twisted in the opposite direction, so being straightened out and more symmetrical will not necessarily 'feel' straighter or better, though this will feel less odd as time goes by and will become associated with the back orders. It is as well to remind the pupil that when the back is down on the couch and flat he or she must not confuse flatness with length and width. A lengthening and widening back will be flat but should in no way be forced down, but a flat back can still be quite shortened and narrowed as well as fixed and 'dead'.

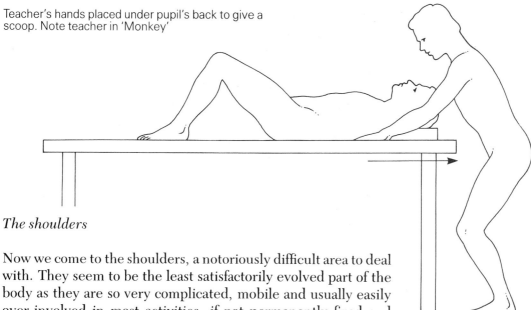

Teacher's hands placed under pupil's back to give a scoop. Note teacher in 'Monkey'

The shoulders

Now we come to the shoulders, a notoriously difficult area to deal with. They seem to be the least satisfactorily evolved part of the body as they are so very complicated, mobile and usually easily over-involved in most activities, if not permanently fixed and distorted. Every other part of the body seems to work beautifully and logically *if* it is well used, but the shoulders seem to be almost the most difficult area to keep under control and use well. Often they are the first area, after the neck, to become grossly interfered with and one of the last areas to become free and improve, but a good teacher should be able to undo all but the most intractable shoulders to some extent, on the couch.

He or she will probably place one hand under a shoulder-blade and with the other will take hold of the shoulder with the fingers resting in the hollow above the collar-bone (clavicle). Again, the pupil should refuse to react to this and will keep his or her attention on leaving the neck and head alone, not allowing them to move to one side or the other, and yet not 'fixing' them in the central position, whilst the shoulder is being manipulated. The teacher should take great care not to disturb this reasonable central alignment. With the hands he or she will then encourage the shoulder to release and widen sideways away from the neck, creating width both across the front and back of the shoulder girdle, with the shoulder-blade possibly moving down the back a little, flat against the rib cage and then dropping down on to the couch.

As there are many ways of interfering with the shoulders: holding them up round the ears, pulling them down and creating

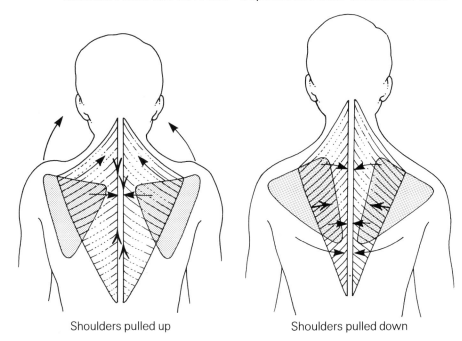

Shoulders pulled up   Shoulders pulled down

pressure into the sides of the rib cage, pulling them forwards or backwards, various combinations of these possibilities with perhaps one up and one down, over-involving them in all sorts of activities like lifting, carrying, reaching, pointing or anything enlisting the arms as well as something as basic as wrong breathing, we need an order to the shoulders that covers most eventualities and 'Shoulder release and widen' comes as near to this as is possible, as most of us are fixing and narrowing in some way or other. We must think of widening both across the front and across the back. If we only widen across the front the probability arises of pulling the shoulder-blades together at the back, creating pressure into a very delicate and important part of the nervous system in this area. This is the sort of thing we are told to do when young: 'Stand up straight, chest out, shoulders back!' and are frequently encouraged to do in 'keep fit' classes. It is highly dangerous. If, however, we only think of widening across the back, the possibility then arises of pulling the shoulders round to the front so that they poke forward in a nasty, hunched, rounded way, and the shoulder-blades probably stick out like wings. This is a common sight.

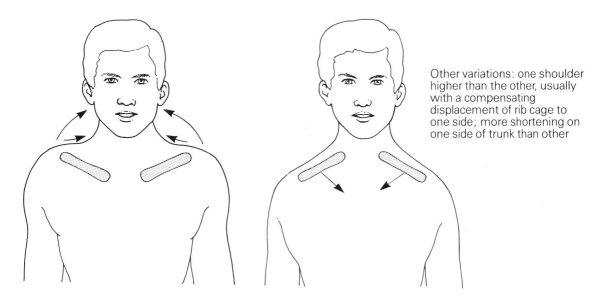

Other variations: one shoulder higher than the other, usually with a compensating displacement of rib cage to one side; more shortening on one side of trunk than other

Collar bones pulled up   Collar bones pulled down

It is a useful idea to think of the line of the collar-bone and the top edge (or 'spine') of the shoulder-blade, similarly placed at the back, making a 'V' shape of bone that needs to release outwards to the side, away from the neck with the point of the 'V' furthest away from the neck. It is not, at this stage, a good idea to think too much about the level of the shoulders as it tends to encourage a pulling down and fixing of the area if they appear to be too high. They must improve in conjunction with the generally improving back, as they will probably need something to relase and widen on to in the way of more tone and support from a good lower and middle back, as well as a possible release of tension in the front of the chest and almost certainly a lot of releasing in the neck. The level also depends frequently on what is going on further down in the trunk, which might well be more contracted down one side than the other. You never know where shoulders are going to end up once they start releasing, but this improvement must be within the context of the generally improving state.

Some teachers might want to turn the head to the side, still resting on the supporting books or pad, whilst working on the shoulders, as this can help encourage a greater releasing and

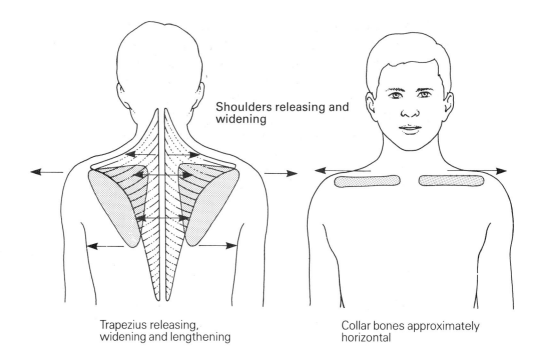

Shoulders releasing and widening

Trapezius releasing, widening and lengthening

Collar bones approximately horizontal

lengthening in the neck and shoulder muscles, particularly the trapezius. In this case the idea of the head being turned must once again be inhibited and attention given more to the means of it being turned than to the end-result, the new place in which it will arrive. In fact keep the three main guiding orders uppermost in the attention and with a free neck and a freely poised head the turn will be easier, possibly involving less muscular activity in the neck and a freer pivot of the head on the top of the spine. It seems to help to think of the pivot being right up in the skull. Even at the end of the movement, when the head has turned, it should not be fixed in the new position but be thought of as in a new resting place with the same order maintained, 'Head forward and up'. It is *not* a correct position for the head, but a *direction*, indicating an absence of everything that is interfering with the free poise and balance of the head which most commonly is pulling it back and down, hence 'Head forward and up'.

Sometimes an order like 'Neck release and lengthen' is useful, thinking of the neck as growing outwards from between the shoulder-blades up into the skull, especially in such a movement as the turning of the head as so often we do the opposite: neck stiffen and shorten. But in the early lessons it is best to stick to the pure form of the Alexander orders so as to lay down clearly a basic grammar which can later be added to for the individual's requirements. Perhaps an order like 'Throat release' would be helpful to some people for a while as part of the more general undoing needed in the neck area, but it is best not to particularise too soon as it only complicates matters, limits the main orders in developing their fullest meaning, and might take away from this vital central attention. However you will see that now we are adding on extra orders, 'Knees to the ceiling' when in the lying position, and 'Shoulders release and widen' as secondary orders.

Absorbing the change

At this stage the basic process is a little like learning to drive. In the early driving lessons you have consciously to think of the sequence in which various activities must be carried out, fastening the seat-belt, putting in the key, turning on the engine, depressing the clutch, going into first gear, and so forth, but after a few lessons this has all become familiar and almost second nature and you tend not to think 'What do I do next?'. However, if you are in a differently arranged car, or if there is a grinding of the gears, you go into the wrong gear, or suddenly someone steps out into the street in front of you, you know immediately what action to take. Because the whole process has been built up recently, very deliberately and consciously, it is as though it immediately comes to the forefront of your attention and you react appropriately. Similarly with the technique, a strict hierarchy of attention must be built up from the start: inhibition, the three main guiding orders to the neck, head and back and then any others that might be appropriate for the next movement or reaction, so that if, for example, you are about to sit or stand you will need to attend to your knees as well, or if you are about to use your arms you will need to attend to the shoulders and arms.

Obviously you cannot go around inhibiting *every* stimulus to act and projecting the string of orders before responding, or you would never get anything done – though you could well do worse. However, with the lessons and the ways in which you should be taught to work on yourself, the whole business should start to get into the system, seemingly hovering at the edge of your attention, so that if you are in a situation that is liable to wreck you in some way, or make you go back into your old bad habits, you should be able to bring the principle to the fore and apply it to that situation and thus deal with it more reasonably. The more the principle is applied the better, as this will stabilise the improvement and refine it, enabling you to take it to a higher or more subtle level.

Here again difficulties can arise: as one becomes more subtly aware so matters can seem to be getting worse, but they never are. It is largely true that the more tense people are the less likely they are to know it. As matters improve one becomes aware of much subtler problems, and so the pupil should be encouraged to realise that this is a healthy state to be in and should not be allowed to become depressed. Often we go through a period when we know we cannot so easily go back into the old bad habits but are not yet secure, comfortable or happy with the better ways, but this is only a passing phase and it is often accompanied by various rewards in the way of pleasanter, if sometimes odd, sensations; though some people can experience a certain amount of discomfort as muscles come into play properly, possibly for the first time, or begin to work in different ways.

As we lose the old bad habits it is often difficult to regain or even recall them, as they were usually built up unconsciously and sometimes they have even disappeared before the pupil was fully aware of them. However we can easily develop new problems. Most people are not only reinforcing their old bad habits all the time but adding on new bad habits as well. With this new way of working one should not only be stabilising the improved use of the self, but be less likely to develop new problems. It is a change of direction in one's life. Instead of progressing down the old slippery slope of mis-use and general deterioration, one should frequently be encouraging the improvement, stabilising and refining, and so gradually raising the 'norm' or level of good use below which one should not fall, even when not thinking about it very consciously, or when in times of crisis there is no time to stop and think. If you are crossing the street and a bus is heading for you, you are not going to stop, inhibit and give your orders, you are going to get out of the way as quickly as possible, and with the work you should have done on yourself in the past, you should be that much better co-ordinated and aware to get out of the way more quickly. Nevertheless modern living often seems designed to wreck us in some way or other so there is always something to be aware of, to inhibit, and to which we can apply the principle. But by now it will probably have become a means of coping and a better way of living, not just something to bring relief or think about when 'relaxing'.

As we adhere to this strict hierarchy of attention through the three main guiding orders plus the extra ones, as and when appropriate, we are building up a total pattern awareness of the body, so that in time we can attend to individual areas without losing the general picture. If we are creating unnecessary tension somewhere, perhaps bracing the knees back too hard, hunching the shoulders or clenching the buttocks, we can do something about these odd spots without losing the total pattern awareness. It is rather like a piece missing from a jigsaw puzzle, we find the piece and complete the picture again. After some time the orders to attend to the neck and head will trigger off a whole sequence of attention to all the parts, so that we do not have laboriously to go through a long string of orders all the time we are thinking about ourselves, though returning to a detailed careful approach will still be necessary if we are in a mess and will continue to be useful when taking the changing process to a more advanced stage.

If there is a problem in some local area of the body it is no use only attending to that part. The Alexander Principle emphasises the importance of bringing about an improved awareness of the total pattern and coordination to the whole structure. If you only attend to the apparent problem, as so often happens in conventional medical treatment, and not to the whole, you tend at best to gain only temporary relief, move the problem around or disguise it, you rarely lose the problem. By sticking to the Alexander 'means whereby', these problems tend often to dissolve or disappear into this improving total pattern and better connected state. It cannot be emphasised enough at this stage that we must keep to this principle, however much it goes against what we have been told in the past, and only after it is firmly established can we be fairly sure that we are both attending to our feet and not losing our heads.

Working on oneself (1)

Try to be aware of what you are doing to yourself in everyday actions

In the early days of having lessons it is asking too much of most of us to apply the technique to difficult situations or complex activities. I usually suggest that pupils start to be aware on a more trivial level; to notice how they are doing certain things around the house or at work for example. Do they pick up the telephone by hunching the shoulder, turn the tap or door knob by fixing the wrist and unnecessarily tensing the arm, do they cut the bread by shifting all the weight to one side and lifting the shoulder? When they clean their teeth do they stiffen the neck, pull back the head, hunch the shoulders, tense the arm, fix the wrist, elbow and shoulder joint, and perhaps also brace back the knees, clench the buttocks, hold the breath and even curve over the washbasin with a bent spine rather than use the hip joints? Such patterns are very common and if we have been doing these sorts of things to ourselves most of our lives they will have become the norm, will feel largely right, and it will be difficult not to do them.

Working to the principle of 'putting as little effort into things as possible' is not a bad idea at this stage. Often the less you are doing means that you are approaching a more appropriate level of effort. Decide perhaps to pick up a cup. Think first of doing nothing and then build up to what is the minimum requirement, probably only a little pressure between the thumb and the fore-finger and raising the arm gently by bending the elbow. Use odd periods of the day when you are not pushed for time and on your own to apply this idea; perhaps when in the kitchen for five minutes making a cup of coffee. Picking up the kettle, taking off the lid, turning on the tap and filling the kettle, plugging it in and switching on, then unscrewing the coffee jar, spooning out the coffee and adding the hot water, sugar and milk: all this involves only hands and arms with the possible need to walk a step or two between kettle and sink, most of the body being in a state of balanced rest. Notice how the shoulders want to be involved, or how you want to shift your weight, brace your knees, hold your breath, clench your buttocks, etc. By working to the principle of doing the minimum you can find out a great deal about yourself, and, as you notice certain of the unnecessary tension patterns, you tend to rely on them less and less and on preconceived ideas of the amount of effort required for these activities.

This state of balanced rest that the body should constantly return to and in which it should remain much more frequently is, alas, something very few of us have or appreciate, as we are often in a rigid or collapsed state, or often a combination of the two extremes, both harmful. It is very common for people to be very rigid in the shoulder or chest areas and very collapsed in the back with over-tensed legs or buttocks for example. As young children we usually have a reasonable instinctive ability to return to this balanced resting state if we have been handled reasonably and are healthy, but we seem to lose this gift quite early on, so to regain it consciously later on in life is going to be very valuable. Notice how young children often seem alert but at ease, taking in everything around them with no apparent strain or need to appear to be concentrating. If children have learned to sit up or stand in their own good time, they will do so effortlessly and, even if they are still quite unsteady when standing or walking and sit down abruptly, they will not jar their spine, as they will still have the natural 'force of levity' which can counteract gravity quite adequately, with the spine reasonably lengthened and flexible, and the muscles supporting it in a good state of balance and the discs between the vertebrae playing their proper cushioning role. The head, which is much heavier in relation to a child's body than to an adult's, will still remain freely poised and nicely balanced. Animals too usually have this good balanced state of rest. Watch a cat as it is about to move, it is quite still and alert but not at all rigid, unless frightened. Most of us tend to move from one rigid position to another rigid position, or from one collapsed state to another, or this combination of the two extremes, very collapsed in some areas but too tense in others. It is as though at the end of a movement we turn off the engine completely, instead of just returning to neutral, and in order to get going again it is as though we have to crank the whole machine into action with some of us seeming to go into reverse before going forward, so much preparatory tension do we make. The importance of regaining 'a state of balanced rest' at frequent intervals is something that I will return to later.

You will need to slow down in order to notice what you are doing to yourself, and most people who lead a busy life need to do so frequently in any case. Often as you slow down you seem to achieve just as much by doing far less. You begin to attend more clearly to the task in hand, and then channel your energy more

Balanced resting state

If only we could keep this beautiful poise

appropriately. You do not waste so much energy nor create so much wear and tear in the process. Often areas of accident proneness, clumsiness, irritability seem to improve. It is as though you are cutting out some of the barriers of tension between yourself and what you are trying to achieve, listen to, take in or learn. This attention to HOW you are doing various things has a great deal to do with a satisfactory learning process. Probably one reason why children learn so much more in the first few years of their lives than in the rest of their lives put together, in most cases, is that they are not blocking out what is going on around them. They are much more receptive and sensitive to stimuli and their environment than later on in life when they are in a state of tension and mis-use that prevents an efficient way of accepting new facts and experiences. They do not have preconceived ideas about life's difficulties or of the amount of effort various activities seem to need. John Dewey, the American educational philosopher, maintained that this approach through the technique and its attention to 'means' rather than 'ends' was vitally important in education, and that the technique stood in the same relationship to education as education did to life. It certainly helps with the learning processes when you attend more to *how* you are doing things than worry too much about the end-result; which brings us to Alexander's concept of 'end-gaining'.

We have all we need. We know how to do all the things necessary to rebuild our environment if we want to. We know how to build rapid transit systems, we know how to get smog out of the air, we know how to build electric power systems that don't pollute. We don't have to imagine or predict new technologies in order to imagine a new type of city; it just needs someone to make up his mind to build it. The only thing no one knows how to do is educate, and – who can tell? – the knowledge about even that might come along one day.

Dr Donald Dunn

In general our reactions on any level tend to be over-quick, frequently there are strong reflex responses present in us and quite early on in life we develop countless automatic, habitual ways of reacting, to which we give no thought and over which we seem to have little control. We are encouraged in this from an early age: to 'jump to it', 'hurry up', 'get on with it' and so on, and then are praised for being the first child to walk, talk, for getting high marks, passing examinations, getting into college, getting a good job, and are judged by how nice a house we have, how big a car, how much we earn. Very little thought either by ourselves or by those who judge us is given to how we might have achieved these ends. There is nothing wrong with having goals and ambitions, they might be highly desirable, but if the means whereby we achieve these ends only produce illness and unhappiness the value of them must be questioned. If we give a little more attention to means, use our intelligence a·little more, we can frequently get just as good results, maybe better, with far less wear and tear, stress and strain, and harm done both to ourselves and those around us. Even an apparently trivial action like getting in and out of a chair can produce untold distortion and harmful pressure in the body, with wasted energy and an exercising of faulty patterns. However, thought and proper attention *can* encourage balance, tone, fluidity, lightness and an exercising of beneficial patterns throughout a better coordinated structure. It will therefore probably be contrary to our usual way of thinking to be told by the teacher that the results at this stage are relatively unimportant, and might be quite novel and refreshing to be encouraged to disregard these results and ends, and to consider the more important 'means whereby' we are going to do anything.

'End-gaining'

This idea can simplify life considerably, and immediately eases some of the burden when all one has to attend to is the next moment or reaction to the next stimulus, cope with that intelligently to the best of one's ability, then go on to the next, and so on. This will usually produce a series of better experiences than we have been used to, which in turn can lead to a greater self-confidence, an enjoyment of 'living in the present', and contentment, but it does conflict at first with one's old ideas and

The 'means whereby'

71

inclinations. We develop bad habits of thought as well as muscular patterns; worry, anxiety and a reliance on too much tension become the norm. We feel we must 'do' something about a situation when all we are doing is getting more agitated and making matters worse. We anticipate crises or worry about things which might never happen or over which we have no control. We go on worrying about things long since past and regret things that went wrong to such an extent that we cannot enjoy the here and now. Even when there is nothing at all to worry about we find problems or anticipate difficulties because of bad experiences in the past. We rely constantly on misconceptions and preconceptions. We try hard to get things right but because we are in a mess we just make matters worse and get more and more depressed and frustrated. By learning to attend with intelligence to a single moment, the next stimulus, we are probably doing the best we can. Crises often do not seem like crises if you are in a good state when you have to deal with them; even if you are aware that it is a crisis you are dealing with, you will at least be able to deal with it more appropriately, without getting so wrecked by it, and from a healthier, stabler state and viewpoint than if you had spent ages anticipating and building up to it, probably having neglected numerous other activities on the way or having dealt with them inefficiently.

'I've always found myself trying to fix other people and I realise you can't do that. Something I found out when I was about 60, I don't know why it took me so long, is not to waste energy trying to make other people be the way you think they ought to be, because you can't control what other people do, only the way you react to what they do. If other people are annoying you, it's not they who are being annoying, it's you who are being annoyed. Don't work on them, work on yourself – it's all so simple.'

Monica Dickens

We are no use to other people if we are in a mess, so contrary to what many people think we do need to attend to ourselves much more than we realise; this is not selfish but entirely practical, providing inhibiting does not become an 'end' in itself but just part of this 'means whereby' we are going to react more appropriately. Great relief and clarity of thought can be gained by this new way of looking at life, so great emphasis will be given in the lessons to this better pattern of thought, the idea of attending to the 'means whereby' rather than to 'end-gaining'. This is an important part of the Technique which is, after all, concerned with finding out what thinking is.

Attending to oneself

The pupil should be encouraged from an early stage to notice HOW he is using himself, but should be discouraged from trying to do anything much about it as yet. Having established a clear understanding of the basic principles of Inhibition and Direction he can however begin to check what is going on and monitor to some extent the state he is in. It is a good idea to use all those odd moments of the day when we are not thinking of anything of particular importance or doing anything special, as when we are waiting for trains or buses, standing in queues, and so on. So start with standing still.

The correct order of attention should always be adhered to.

• Notice the neck and check that it is not unduly stiffened or tight.

• Then the head – is it pulled back or dropped forward or to one side. Is the chin poking forward or pulled in? You might not yet know very clearly what you are doing, but with the teacher's help and perhaps the aid of a mirror you will gradually become aware of some of the grosser forms of interference. Imagine that your head is like a 'ping-pong' ball balancing on a jet of water, like those targets you see in shooting galleries at fairs. It is rather as though the spine were the jet of water shooting up and falling away like the shoulders, with the head perched lightly on the top.

• Then notice the back – are the shoulders unduly hunched, pulled back together or poking round to the front with 'winged' shoulder-blades? Is the lower back thrown in and swayed forward with the pelvis tilted and the tummy protruding? Or is the breast-bone held up tightly? Are you poking forward with the upper section of the spine, dropping from between the shoulder-blades or the 'hump' area? Are the buttocks very clenched or is one hip out to the side? All such likely tendencies will interfere with a properly lengthened and widened back.

• Now notice the arms. How do they hang? Are the elbows perhaps pulled back and into the side of the body, or are they held out from the side rather like a penguin? The former indicates a twist in the shoulder joint, tense shoulders, and often an over-contraction of the inner part of the upper arm, and the latter usually over-developed shoulders, muscle-bound and arms that are fixed. The arms should hang freely with the elbows slightly away from the sides of the body and the hands hanging with the backs more or less facing forward slightly in front of the thigh. This will happen naturally as the shoulders come undone and the arms become less tense, but it is no bad thing to encourage them to hang like this, even though at this stage it will feel odd, perhaps even a little 'round-shouldered', eventually it will feel quite comfortable especially when the shoulders are sorted out and there is more of a back to support them in a free state.

• What about the legs? If you are standing 'straight', do you brace the knees back, or do you often stand with one leg braced and the other bent so that the hip goes out to the side? It is common to confuse a braced leg with the muscles tightened and shortened, and a straight leg where the muscles are properly balanced and there is no undue pressure into the joints. Not only are the knees too often braced back but they are frequently pulled together, 'squinting', at each other through a shortening of the inner part of the upper leg. Sportsmen and dancers can often be doing the opposite, pushing the legs apart, and all of these possibilities will not only interfere with the balance in the antagonistic muscle pulls in the leg but will almost certainly be encouraging a tendency to fix in the hip joints, tighten the ankles, create wrong pressures in the feet with the possibility of fallen arches or flat feet or even a tendency to walk too much on the outside of the foot. Inevitably there will be too much weight thrown on to the ball of the foot and, most ruinously of all perhaps, it will adversely affect the back, probably encouraging the buttocks to be too tight, often the lower back to be thrown in, and certainly in some way shortened and fixed. The orders to the legs therefore should be like all the other orders, the opposite of what is most liable to happen. The most common tendency is to pull them back and together, hence the order 'knees forward and away'. This is merely to check that the opposite is not happening and should not be confused with bracing them apart or a bent knee. They should not be 'turned out' as in ballet, and it is perfectly possible to have a quite rigid bent knee. If this new condition, which is brought about by not doing the old thing, brings you up off your arches, perhaps you need this even if it feels odd. If it takes you too much on to the outside of your feet, however, you will need to think your knees 'apart' but your inner ankle bones 'together', which in time will greatly increase the flexibility of the ankles. If you really do not know what you are doing to your legs, go ahead and brace them back, then let them go with the slightest flexing of the knee and a rotation outwards if they are not already 'away' from each other, keeping the 'forward' thought going as they move slightly 'away'.

Releasing into a better state

Having gone through this detailed sequence of attending to yourself you can then begin to release certain areas that are over-tense, within the context of keeping this string of orders in mind so that you are not losing what is going on at the top end of the body even when you consider your legs. If the breast-bone is 'held', then you might be able to let it go a little, but only so that you are gaining something more in the way of extra length and width in the back, the area under the shoulder-blades in this case. As you consider the lower back you might also need to attend to the legs in the way I have just described, and this might allow you to release some of the clenching in the buttocks if it is appropriate, perhaps ironing out any excessive curve there might be or releasing any tightness. The bottom of the spine (coccyx) might drop but this must only happen so as to allow for more lengthening in the spine, mainly upwards towards the skull. This will be the start of a more reasonable way of using the back, developing tone and stability and a generally more 'lively' back. This in turn will allow for easier releasing of the shoulders, as they will then have a good back on to which they can release and into which they can become integrated, as there will no longer be such a need for them to be 'held'. This will also allow for any necessary further releasing in the chest, a freeing of the breathing and even more freedom in the neck. So by having started by attending to yourself from the top downwards, letting the knees release can effect an improvement in the balance and alignment in the whole structure upwards; thus a kind of circular attention process is going on. It is permissible to make adjustments, and we frequently have to at this stage though less and less often as things improve, *providing they are inhibited first and then linked into the Ordering sequence*, and encourage greater releasing, which must always be into a definite direction, length, and/or width, NOT into a state of collapse.

Pupils are always asking in their first lesson what they can do about themselves, and frankly there isn't very much at all, at this stage. Even if you could wave a wand and turn them into some perfect specimen they would not like it, as it would feel so alien to them, so unlike what they had been used to. However an area that can be attended to quite early on is the common practice of crossing the knees when seated. This is a difficult habit to break and yet can be extremely harmful. Apart from interfering with the circulation in this area, if the knees are constantly crossed it is almost impossible to build up full support, and maintain the tone and stability that should be present in the lower back muscles. If you do not have this the lower back will become weak and vulnerable and all the supporting work that should be going on in this area will have to be done elsewhere, most likely in the shoulders, front of the chest or neck, quite possibly all three, and reinforcing yet again the common practice of interfering in these

Crossing knees is ruinous, but is almost universal in western society

76

parts. A vicious circle is being perpetuated: the big supporting muscles in the back are being mis-used; this encourages an over-use of the secondary muscles up above, which allows the lower back to become weak and vulnerable, and the neck, shoulders and chest over-tense. Muscles which should only come into play for certain activities are permanently tightened, and the big supporting muscles in the lower back are either flaccid and not working at all or are over-working and pulled out of balance.

Crossing one knee over the other tends to encourage one side of the pelvis to be raised, thus creating a sideways curve of the spine, a shortening on one side of the trunk and an imbalance in the lower back muscles, also jammed-up hip joints. The deep inner muscles from the lower back into the thigh (psoas) will be frequently over-contracted and cause further shortening, collapse or a fixing in this area. It is permissible to cross the ankles with the knees slightly apart, and if ladies feel that they must keep their knees together when wearing dresses they can do so in time without actually pulling them together and losing the support of a good lower back which is well-toned without being fixed. In no way can you maintain good balance by crossing the knees, and without this it is impossible to have good muscle tone.

If the lower back is not working properly, which is common, a kind of division occurs in the body's structure. It is as though we cut ourselves in half somewhere in this area. Sometimes the separation of the top half from the bottom half of the body can be a little higher up in the middle back as well. This lack of connection happens through collapsing in the lower back, throwing it forward or curving sideways, tightening too much, perhaps through over-straightening, developing a twist in the chest or pelvis, and various combinations of these possibilities. The shoulders become over-tense, jammed into the neck or pulled up to the ears, often the chest too, and the neck and head jammed together and this whole area becomes a fixed mass; and the buttocks can be too tight, the hips fixed and the legs mis-used so that the pelvis and legs become another jammed-up mass. It is a good idea, therefore, to think of the shoulders and the pelvis as part of the back, comprising a nicely integrated unit, not solid but stable; so that the hip joints and shoulder joints are the four corners of the main rectangular working area of the body, with the arms and legs freely releasing out of the four corners, and with the head as the balancing mechanism on top of the whole structure. And remem-

Crossing your ankles does no harm

ber: the spine goes up into the skull and a good back depends largely on a well-lengthened spine. So do not think of the back as stopping between the shoulder-blades. So you have the dynamically poised head on the top of the lengthening spine, and the four corners of the trunk, out of which are releasing the four main limbs.

Crossing the knees is often linked to other patterns of tension

Body image

A diagrammatic idea of oneself can sometimes be useful to pupils. But to visualise or imagine oneself only in this way is going to limit the eventual full meaning of the orders which should in time trigger off much more than an image: rather a whole world of experience in the sensory area too, as well as monitoring what is going on at the present or is about to happen. Images, although a rather fashionable way of working, usually get in the way. They are a barrier to the immediacy of the nervous system working through the orders. However, it is often no bad thing to have a better image of ourselves, related to what we can be like, rather than how we are used to seeing ourselves: an idealised image, if you like, that we are working towards, which will help us to inhibit old habits of mis-use and encourage the improved manner of use.

Over the years we see ourselves in photographs, on video or home movies, in mirrors as we try on clothes; we are told that we

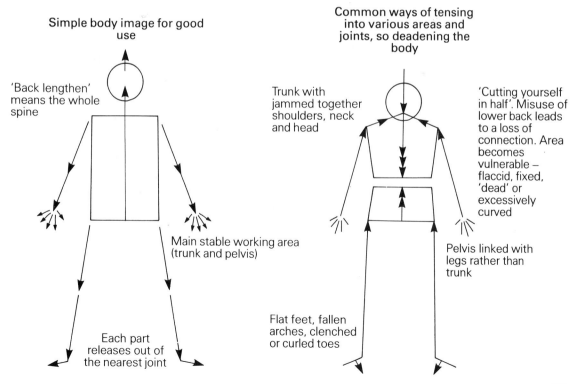

Simple body image for good use

'Back lengthen' means the whole spine

Main stable working area (trunk and pelvis)

Each part releases out of the nearest joint

Common ways of tensing into various areas and joints, so deadening the body

Trunk with jammed together shoulders, neck and head

'Cutting yourself in half'. Misuse of lower back leads to a loss of connection. Area becomes vulnerable – flaccid, fixed, 'dead' or excessively curved

Pelvis linked with legs rather than trunk

Flat feet, fallen arches, clenched or curled toes

look fat or thin or chirpy or depressed, and so on. We see people around us whom we suspect we look like; we are told that we are the image of our parents or some other member of the family, or we try to copy people we like the look of. All this creates in our minds an image of how we look. Unfortunately most of those people with whom we identify, or the images we receive of ourselves are more often than not associated in some way with mis-use; people who are tired, collapsed, rigid, hunched, braced, twisted, bent, fixed, depressed, pulling themselves down, and far more rarely do we see examples of good use. Even the models we are supposed to emulate and admire, or the states to which we are supposed to aspire, are more to do with fashion, whim, or subjective ideas of beauty and health.

Gradually through the lessons, therefore, a new body image must be constructed. Working in front of a mirror is useful here, and most teachers will, like Alexander, use a mirror frequently, though many people are reluctant to be confronted with what they really look like, and prefer their imaginary idea of themselves, or simply avoid thinking about it. Learning to observe yourself is important however, recognising symmetry, even if you do not yet possess it, and a good alignment, as well as mis-use and interference, and the pupil who really wants to change will appreciate this. Encouragement from the teacher will help, showing you how much better you look when in a good state, pointing out the difference when you are not pulling down or perhaps hunching up; a mirror will give you an idea of what is possible, something you can see and ally to the new feelings. We are not trying to achieve through this way of working some perfect form into which we can all be moulded – there is no way that can happen – nor are we taking away anything of the individual's essential self. What will happen will be a gradual discarding of those patterns and attitudes through which we disguise our real selves, behind which we hide and with which we armour ourselves. The aggressive machismo or over-sexy wiggle are not necessary if you feel secure in yourself and do not feel the need to impress, and if we choose to adopt such attitudes at least they will be conscious, and something we choose to use, rather than barriers between the real self and the image we wish to project.

What we look like depends to a large extent on our natural physical type and the only thing we can do about that is to make the best of it by using ourselves as well as possible. The development of the embryo determines what type we are: thin (ectomorph), fat (endomorph) or muscular (mesomorph). Everybody is a mixture of all these major elements, but often one can predominate and if it does so radically then it is likely that that person will acquire the disadvantage of that particular type. The extremely thin person will often have a long vulnerable back, might be over-quick in reacting, often unstable and sometimes neurotic. The very fat person can be slow and lethargic, heavy and stodgy, depressed both physically and mentally. The over-muscled type can become muscle-bound and very fixed in the body and perhaps in certain mental attitudes.

The lucky ones are those who are a good balance of the three main types, often the great dancers and sportsmen are in this category, though the more erratic performers will frequently lack this balance, and, of course, they will often need to build up more strength and stamina than the average person for their particular activity. This will not necessarily allow them to function more efficiently in general however, rather the opposite. If you are lucky enough to be a good balance of the three main elements you will tend to have the advantages of each type, the figure of the slimmer people, the stability of the fat and the strength and tone of the muscular.

There are ways of determining one's physical make-up by measuring fat and bony structure, but it is easy to disguise our natural type. We lose weight through worrying, or over-eat and gain weight for the same reason. We overwork or overindulge; health problems and many other factors must be considered. But by using ourselves well and working in an Alexander way over a lengthy period we begin to discover just what type we are and make the best of it, encouraging those elements we lack. The fatties will need to develop tone and lightness in the body, the thin ones greater stability, economy of effort and greater control of reactions, and the muscly ones a releasing into a more fluid state in which their energy is used more freely. The USE element is something we can really attend to and do something about whatever we've been given at birth, so that we can make the most of what we have and encourage efficient functioning, without being so erratic and succumbing to our weaknesses.

Types of physique

General attention

I frequently tell my pupils to think about themselves at first in fairly general terms, even though a detailed analysis and synthesis are taking place at the same time in the lessons. This detailed attention to oneself is important but most pupils cannot think in this way for long periods in the earlier stages of re-education, although it becomes easier with practice. This restructuring of the body is a complicated undoing and rebuilding process which takes time, is different for each of us, and has to be carried out at the right speed for the individual concerned. Certain general tips can nevertheless be useful: suggestions like 'Each movement is a chance to release and lengthen with the head leading', 'Think upwards for a downwards movement' and suchlike seem to help many pupils. 'Think of each part of yourself releasing and lengthening out of the nearest joint' is another such idea, especially as most of us seem to do the opposite: we tend to pull each part of ourselves into the nearest joint. The head gets jammed back and down by a stiffened neck, the neck and the head are pulled into the trunk, the shoulders are held rigidly and pulled into the neck and often up to the ears, the arms are pulled into the shoulder joints, with the elbows and wrists fixed and the fingers clenched, each vertebra is pressing on to the next one with the spine shortened and the rib cage held and the breathing restricted, the legs are fixed in the hip joints, the knees braced, the ankles fixed and probably the toes clenched. In cold or wet weather you see people standing waiting for buses or cycling along actually doing many of these things in a very obvious fashion, as if the huddled, fixed, tensing of the body will make them drier or warmer. In fact it probably makes them colder as they interfere so much with the circulation. It is quite obvious to the teacher that people are in the main less tense in warm weather, though we tend to be doing these sorts of things to ourselves much of the time in some way or other, and simply by thinking in opposite terms we seem to do them much less. It is good general preventive attention. The wear and tear to the structure from such practices is enormous, highly damaging, and a definite contributory factor to many ailments. Most headaches are caused by unnecessary tension, as is much of the pain in arthritis, in digestive and countless other problems. The only reason people feel like tensing in the cold and wet is because they then cannot actually 'feel' just how cold or wet they are. They deaden the body through tension.

Feelings

When we tense our bodies, or indeed mis-use them in any way, we interfere with the freedom and flexibility in the joints, and also certain receptors that are situated there. It is from this that problems can develop. Tension starts, of course, in the muscles which are controlled by the nervous system; messages from the brain reach the muscle through the motor nerves. Almost half of these messages are received in the muscle by a mechanism called the muscle spindle, which was only discovered during Alexander's lifetime, and which is responsible for the feedback we get from the muscles through the sensory nerves. There are thousands of these muscle spindles in each muscle, surrounded by the general overlying muscle tissue, and it has been discovered quite recently that there are many more of these spindles in the neck muscles than in any other area, further substantiating Alexander's claim that the neck is the key to sorting oneself out. This mechanism is also responsible for a large part of a muscle's ability to lengthen, not just the lengthening that happens when we stop shortening a muscle but a voluntary lengthening that can come under our conscious control. This is the area of ordering that has frequently to be taken on trust until the muscles are re-educated so that the spindles are reactivated. This mechanism also connects to that part of the brain through which we are conscious of our environment.

This very over-simplified explanation of muscle physiology is important when we consider how muscles work, but the most important fact is that this whole mechanism does not function properly when we mis-use our bodies. The unbalanced patterns in the muscles, called dystonic patterns, that are caused by over-tension, hunching, bracing, twisting, collapsing, when either still or in movement, cut out this mechanism and the brain receives faulty messages, half-messages, or often no messages at all. The two-way message service from brain to body and back again has broken down. Modern living is so complex, hectic, and in many ways so unnatural – we are wildly over-stimulated mentally and wrongly stimulated physically, sitting as we do for long periods at office desks or machines, cooped up in cars, rushing around leading over-busy lives or crushed together in trains and buses, frustrated and angry as we cope inadequately

The joys of modern urban living. Why do we do it?

with what should be a full, rich life. It is almost as though the brain is telling the neck to stiffen for everything we do, every reaction, movement, activity, and the free poise and balance of the head to be interfered with, likewise the back. As we are projecting the orders however, these harmful patterns begin to come under our conscious control and we tend to reinforce them less and less, allowing the muscles in this most important area, through which goes the central nervous system, Alexander's Primary Control, to work better in a more balanced fashion, and allowing other areas to function more reasonably as a result. The whole muscle spindle mechanism is awakened, endowing us with a more reliable means of monitoring ourselves through an improved sensory awareness. The orders are at this time becoming linked to this new improvement in the kinaesthetic sense. Gradually we are developing a whole new way of feeling, in which we are not so imprisoned that we cannot use our brains. We all rely on our feelings all the time but we do not have to be so glued to them that we cannot think

84

properly. What is more, feelings can be re-educated through good use to be more reliable.

We all have problems similar to the one Alexander had to face when he was acting. He could see that the old ways of using his body were harmful and probably causing him to lose his voice, and yet the new way, whilst it looked better, did not *feel* better. He felt insecure, slack and disorientated when he was not relying on the old tension patterns, strain and effort that he was employing to recite. Pupils might well have similar feelings. Of course the new ways might also feel much better, often in the lessons the pupils will experience feelings of ease, lightness and general well-being, pleasant feelings that they will wish to maintain. Yet the old habits will at first be so strong that they will inevitably resort to them outside the lessons, and at this stage there will be strong reflex patterns which they can do little about on their own. As matters change the improvement will be quickly absorbed as it is only related to what should have been going on anyway and something that we have been interfering with. So what might have felt wonderful and novel in the early lessons might well feel quite ordinary after a time. Even the best 'used' of us, however, tends to 'feel' better after a lesson. Modern living is so likely to wreck us that we need frequent reminding of the principle and experience. Some pupils 'feel' very little, they might well be able to observe in a mirror how they have changed, how they have apparently grown, become more symmetrical or spread their weight differently, they might even have lost some ache or pain, but apart from that do not 'feel' different. Many pupils' bodies are quite 'dead', but even these can gradually be awakened and become lively and efficient. Nevertheless people vary tremendously, and although most pupils will feel better, some will feel wrong or odd, and others will not feel anything at all. This problem of 'feeling' can be a difficult one and one which Alexander frequently discusses in his books, referring to a 'debauched kinaesthesia', faulty sensory awareness, or unreliable feelings.

As we cannot really trust our feelings after the best part of a lifetime of mis-use, we have to do as Alexander did, and learn to trust the principles of Inhibition and Direction. When inhibiting we are less likely to reinforce old bad habits and when directing or ordering properly we are encouraging some degree of improvement. We cannot hope to bring about an improved, unfamiliar state of change by trusting old, familiar, faulty feelings that are associated with mis-use. By and large what we have been doing to ourselves feels right because it feels familiar, even if we are aware at some level or other that it is not right, consequently the new, better but unfamiliar state can feel wrong. If you are used to wearing your head to one side and the teacher straightens it up it will probably feel over to the other side. Likewise if the teacher corrects a twist in the chest, pelvis or neck you will almost certainly feel twisted in the opposite direction. However, the more frequently you are reminded of the better state the less odd you will feel, but most of our feelings in these areas are very deeply ingrained, and, if we can deal with these deeply-rooted bad habits and faulty feelings, we are encouraging a major change in our lives. As well as learning to trust the orders we can, like Alexander, check what we are doing to ourselves through various objective means. We too can use a mirror to observe what is going on and, as we work on ourselves lying down on what will presumably be a flat floor or couch, we can begin to assess what state the back is in. We will certainly have a better objective idea of it than in the upright position when we will be employing our feelings mainly to check it. Once again it must be emphasised that a flat back will not necessarily be a lengthened and widened back, although the latter will be flat. However a flat surface will encourage a beneficial releasing into something approaching greater length and width: it is something to let go on to without collapsing. Similarly working against a wall can be a useful, more objective means of checking a reasonable alignment in various parts of the structure and I will describe these ways of working later on.

It is helpful to most pupils for the teacher to explain in some detail why the new experiences can feel strange or wrong and why improvement does not necessarily always feel better. To encourage pupils to appreciate that the subtler awareness of deeply seated habits is real progress and a healthy state in which to be, will usually help them through this temporarily disturbing phase of changing, after which they will almost certainly be using themselves better; the odd feelings are a good sign and an indication of real change.

Some pupils go through periods when they feel they are making no progress at all, and this too can be a good sign. Sometimes we need to absorb the change, the body needing to stabilise its improved state, and it is as though we are going along a plateau while this is happening, getting ready for the next breakthrough. Sometimes also we seem to come back to the same old problems time and time again, but this too can be good and a sign of more awareness. Usually the problem will be at a deeper level as we once again cope with it. It is rather like an upward spiral of awareness where we confront subtler versions of the same problems, the opposite of the more usual journey downwards, constantly reinforcing old problems.

Although certain muscles will be flaccid and under-used at the outset of lessons, with most of us many muscles will be overworked and shortened much of the time. Basically, almost anything that encourages muscles to release and lengthen and the muscles spindle mechanism to be reactivated will be valuable at this stage, and work on the couch or floor will be most helpful. With increasing experience of getting back to a balanced resting state we will begin to move from a good starting point more frequently and will thereby bring into play a more balanced use of the muscles within the next activity, gently encouraging the body into better patterns, spreading the work more appropriately, and in fact exercising the body in the most natural way possible, using certain areas more but properly while other parts become less involved.

One of the main reasons for people losing height as they get older is this constant over-contraction of muscles and inability to allow them to return to the lengthened, resting state. A healthy elastic quality in the muscles is being encouraged by releasing – and muscles are actually stronger in this lengthened state. Then by using oneself more reasonably this builds up into improved tone. We also tend to lose height as the day goes on, being busy, getting tired and lapsing into mis-use. Through an awareness of good use we can prevent much of this too and deal with it more reasonably. Most of us regain a better lengthened state after a good night's sleep but after years of mis-use muscles lose the ability to return to this state readily through rest. A vicious circle ensues as mis-use encourages tiredness and inefficiency, and they in their turn encourage grosser mis-use; so this constant attention to releasing and lengthening is vitally important if we wish to continue to function well and happily.

Whilst on the subject of muscle-functioning, it has recently been suggested that the loose connective tissue in the body can be destroyed through mis-use: a gradual silting up of muscles and loss of elasticity develops, surrounding areas come to be used wrongly as required work from the destroyed area becomes rerouted. As a compensation even further limitation of the useful life of the new area occurs, with a further decline in healthy functioning. Improved use will to a large extent stop this vicious circle of deterioration and so the slippery slope of mis-use and consequent malfunctioning down which we are sliding can be reversed into an upward climb towards improved use with all its attendant rewards.

This change of direction in life is one of the most important gifts that the technique has to offer, and however slow the progress, providing it is in the upward, improving direction, the gap between what we would have been and what we now are is ever-widening. We cannot do very much about the atmospheric pressure, the state of the economy, we cannot completely stop the aging process, or change other people directly, but we can attend to how we cope with them and the myriad other problems in life. At least we are attending, to the best of our ability, to those areas of our life that we can directly influence.

As we are working in this way we are directly sorting out the nervous system through the ordering process, the musculature is being improved through manipulation and this affects the bony structure and alignment of the body with the attendant improvement in functioning of the major organs, breathing circulation, the change in balance and alignment, and all that goes towards an improved manner of use. So, you see, a great many areas of our lives can be affected for the better through this work.

Working on oneself (2)

Lying down

After several sessions on the couch most pupils should be encouraged to start working on themselves in this way at home. It is enormously useful in many areas. After a number of lessons the pupil will be using movements to bring about certain improvements, and often it is within a movement that the greatest change and most dramatic or dynamic improvement can take place, because it is in movement that the pupil will most strongly reinforce old patterns. If he can learn to inhibit the old way of moving and direct himself in the new manner before and during a movement, he can bring about a definite improvement even if as yet it doesn't feel better or is imperceptible to the untrained eye. The 'lying down work', although not so dynamic, is nevertheless invaluable, and usually enjoyable.

You can apply this when you wake up in the morning, it might get you going well from the start rather than taking hours to function reasonably, and get rid of some of the stiffness acquired from being in odd positions while asleep. Similarly when you go to bed, it can help get rid of some of the tensions of the day.

It is a good idea perhaps to re-read the section 'Working on a Couch' (pp. 53–65), as working on oneself lying down aims to achieve the same sorts of benefits and effects. Even if you do not seem to gain as much benefit from working on your own, it is nevertheless important to do it as most of the time we cannot have a teacher to rely on. The teacher, in any case, cannot do the REAL work for us; he can only guide, advise and speed up the changing process, but in the final analysis it is up to us to keep it going and apply it.

If you do not have a flat couch, choose a carpeted floor to work on. Too soft a surface, like a bed, will not be so beneficial. Place the books for the head to rest on. It is important to use the first lying down movement to gain at the very least some extra length in the back. Take it slowly and attend to yourself through inhibiting the idea and directing yourself properly as I have previously described. There are only a few movements involved in this area of work but each must be inhibited before being carried out and the guiding orders projected so that the right kind of preparatory attention is being given and then maintained throughout the actual movement so as to bring about some degree of improvement. Lying down provides a chance to release into a lengthened state, rather than collapsing into flatness or forcing the back down. You can, if necessary, release and lengthen out of any tendencies you might have to shorten more on one side of the body than the other, or to undo any twist. If you have been made familiar with such problems by your teacher, now is the opportunity to do something about them, but be sure you do not over-compensate by going to the opposite extreme. Uncurl, with the lower back arriving first, then the middle back, then the shoulders, the neck dropping back but *not* jamming the head back as it arrives last of all on the books. You will become adept at positioning them correctly with practice.

Having lain down do not immediately start to move things around or 'correctly position' yourself. Check by going round the orders what you are doing to yourself. As mentioned before you can often find little areas of tension that can be let go of simply by ceasing to hold on, and by attending in this way.

- Is the head, perhaps, pressed back unduly on to the books?
- Can the neck drop back a little?
- Is the front of the chest held?
- Is the lower back arched up more than absolutely necessary?
- How have the arms and legs arrived?
- Are the knees pulled together?

Real undoing can happen as you check such possibilities.

If you feel you have really lost your head when moving and have arrived with the chin stuck up and the head pulled back into the books, it means you stopped ordering at some point and you will obviously need to do something about it. However in any adjustment you realise to be necessary, stop first and give your orders. Having inhibited the possibility of bringing into play old muscle patterns, and then through the orders attended to the total pattern of the body, any adjustment you now make is likely to be better than if you had merely immediately arranged yourself mechanically. You are more likely to be bringing into play an appropriate use of the muscles, in this case in the neck, a more balanced way of using them for the movement, and less likely to be using too much muscular activity. It is more like a releasing

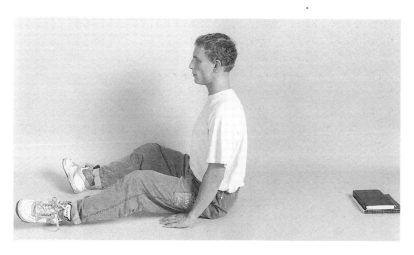

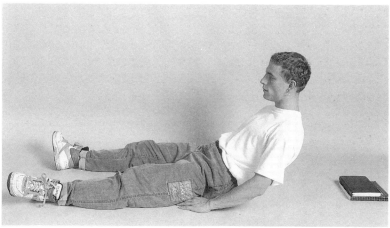

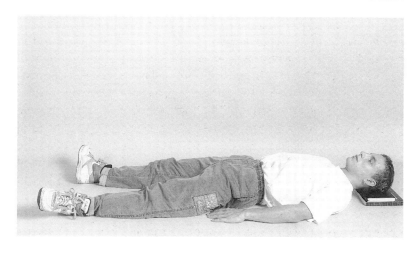

When lying down, let the spine uncurl smoothly, gaining length as you move, with neck arriving before the head

into the better state than merely repositioning yourself. The frequent attention to the three main guiding orders will help any adjustment to be one that becomes part of an improving total-pattern awareness and not just a local rearrangement of some part. Attention to the back orders will often allow for more support to be gained in this area, which will in turn allow for more freedom in the neck. It is as though you will be lying more on your back and less on your head. When lying it is often useful to think of the neck dropping back to the floor or couch with the head merely resting on its support, not pressed into the books or pad. This can help separate the two areas and ease any tightening in the area at the base of the skull, where the spine goes up into it, helping with freedom in the neck and as though creating more space or letting in a bit of air between the two parts. Paradoxically, parts are better connected when there is space between them.

This attention to the main orders, and therefore to an improving TOTAL pattern in the body cannot be over-emphasised. In any adjustment it is vitally important. If you notice when upright that your shoulders are up round your ears, for example, do not just yank them down as pulled down shoulders are just as bad as hunched up ones, and often more difficult to sort out. Stop and order, adding on the order, 'shoulder release and widen', to the three main ones, and then let the shoulders go. A real releasing is more likely to come about this way and the shoulders encouraged to become better integrated into a generally improving back.

As mentioned earlier, the arms should arrive with the elbows away from the side of the trunk and with the hands facing down to the floor, or they can be placed on the chest or tummy. The legs should be straight out with the feet rather wider apart than the pelvis, and with a rotation of the thigh and knees outwards, away from each other, but not forced apart, just rolling easily outwards under their own weight. Quite obviously you have got to 'do' some of these things, they will not necessarily at this stage happen 'naturally' or by magic, or – as one book about the technique suggested – through the 'life force'. If the desirable relationing of one part to another is not present you will probably have to move or adjust to allow it to happen (but this must always be within the context of inhibiting and ordering; it might then well be a kind of 'undoing'). The problems diminish as time goes on and you improve. Free shoulders, for example, will allow the arms to hang and fall in the right way: likewise more freedom in the hips will

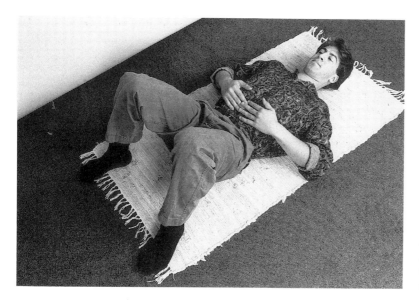

This is one of the most basic ways of working on yourself to bring about fundamental change

allow the legs to arrive as I have described, and with the various other ways of working on the back that will be undertaken in the lessons you will be more and more likely to arrive on the floor with more length and width in this area, but this lying-down movement in itself should be encouraging such a state.

Check also the front of the chest, the breast-bone area. If you were breathing out when moving you would be less likely to have fixed this, but if you find on arrival that you have been holding it up then it is a good idea to release it. Sometimes a good sigh can help here or a mixture of a groan and a sigh. The resonance produced by the groan helps the breast-bone to move and the sigh makes sure it is a releasing movement and not some way of forcing the front of the chest down.

After checking all these possibilities on arrival you will now need to move your legs, first one then the other, with the knees bent up towards the ceiling, for the good reasons mentioned earlier. Give yourself the stimulus to move one leg. Inhibit any automatic, habitual tendencies and check that the neck, head and back are left alone by attending to the main guiding orders. You have now given yourself the right kind of preparatory attention and probably done as much about yourself at this point as you can, so now you may 'give consent' to the movement you first inhibited, or from which you withheld consent. Keeping the directions going, allow it to happen by doing the absolute minimum. To move the leg requires minimal muscular activity, providing the back is ideally lengthened and widened and therefore fully supported by the floor. As this is quite likely not to be the case at this stage, you will probably be doing more than the ideal amount of work, so just do as little as possible. The less you are doing the better, it is more likely to be approaching the appropriate amount of effort.

Notice as you make the movement whether or not you disturb the structure in any way. Did you pull back your head and press it into the books, raise the chest, arch the back, take the pelvis round to one side, or hold your breath? If so, it does not matter too much providing you know you are doing these things, so that the next time you make this movement you will know more clearly what to inhibit, unnecessarily disturbing these parts less, and so over a period the movement should become more and more economical, with eventually no disturbance of the upper part of the body and only this minimal muscular activity to raise the knees. When the leg arrives with the knee bent – the hip-bone (top of iliac crest), middle of knee-cap, front of ankle and gap between big toe and the next one making a straight line – then direct the 'Knee to the ceiling' so that the leg is neither jamming down into the hip joint, nor down on to the ankle or arch, nor should it be braced out to the side or pulling in towards the other leg, flopping about or rigid. It should be in a lightly balanced state, free in the hip and in the ankle. The hip joint, by the way, is not at the front of the pelvis where the leg makes an angle with the pelvis just below the hip-bone, but deep into the side, lower down and further back than the hip-bone, where the thigh-bone fits into a ball-and-socket joint in the pelvis. This is a common misconception. It is important to know where the joint actually is, as this is where we tend to fix a great deal and cause untold harm through mis-use.

As you move the second leg, go through the same procedure, bearing the above in mind, but this time not only will you need to keep the main orders going but you will have to consider the first leg through the 'Knee to the ceiling' order, so that it should remain undisturbed. They should work separately from each other. When moving the legs, general attention, such as thinking of the back being well-supported by the floor and the leg releasing OUT of the hip for the movement, can be helpful. Finally you can

94

include both legs in the sequence of orders to bring them into the picture, though the neck/head/back relationship will continue to be the most important area of attention, and the 'Knees to the ceiling' direction will help to take care of most things that can go wrong with the legs in this new place, as well as encouraging a new lightness, balance and tone in the leg muscles, greater freedom in the joints and a better connection with the lower back where it should now be easier to release.

You will not be able, on your own, to gain as much length and width in the back as the teacher can by putting his or her hands under your shoulders and then down your back and giving you a 'scoop'. However, with the legs up, you will find the lower back dropping down more easily if it is not already doing so, and this extra contact with the surface will allow you to release as best you can over the surface on which you are lying, though, once again, it is not flatness we are aiming for but more length and width, so it is most important to use the first lying-down movement as much as possible to encourage this. As matters improve in the back you should find that you are lying on more of the back than when you started, and more evenly as it releases, not just on odd spots as is often the case early on; but lightly spreading like mercury, not rigidly flattened. As you cannot give yourself a 'scoop', you will gain most of your length in the back through an adjustment to the pelvis, as well as using the initial lying-down movement. This extra length will help stabilise the pelvis in with the rest of the back and help eliminate the common tendency to disconnect, or 'cut yourself in half', in the lower back region, so this pelvic adjustment is very useful.

With many pupils much of this right sort of extra contact with the surface will be in this area, where many of the large supporting muscles become tight and shortened, and will depend on an adjustment in the pelvic region. This should be undertaken by yourself on your own, with the greatest care and attention. Placing the hands under the buttocks to move the bottom part of the pelvis down the floor away from the upper part of the trunk, and thereby gaining more length in this area is often quite a relief, and will allow you to release more of the lower back down to the floor, which will in turn help release other parts of the back. This manoeuvre can wreck your shoulders, and they are generally much more difficult to deal with in the long term than the lower back (although lower back pain is probably more common than

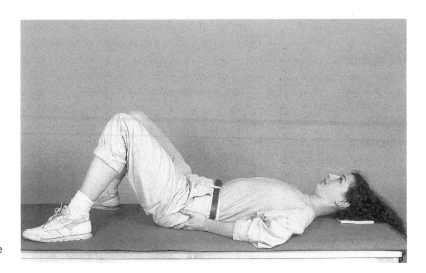

The lower back is lengthened by easing the base of the pelvis carefully away from the top of the spine

shoulder pain); and take much more sorting out. There is no point in wrecking the more difficult area to gain a little relief in the more-easily-dealt-with area. Most pupils will merely tip the pelvis and flatten the back without necessarily gaining the needed length, or they will put the pelvis into what feels like the right position or into a position that feels comfortable, and this is likely to be what they are used to, not what they really need, and is liable to reinforce any habitual twist or tendency to asymmetry. Once again it is the problem of not being able to trust your feelings. As the teacher gives you more and more experience of what is needed, you will begin to realise what is desirable. If this adjustment is attempted it must be with all these possibilities in mind: do not wreck the shoulders, so keep the 'Shoulder release and widen' idea going, be aware of habitual twists and shortenings, and especially keep in mind the requirement of extra length in the lower back as you move the pelvis and link it on to the main orders.

It is often a good idea to come back again to this adjustment after five or ten minutes of lying down. You will frequently find that there is yet more length to be gained in this area once things have really begun to settle and release. You can do it with the knees apart or together, but if the latter then you must once again project the main orders in order to leave the top part of the body undisturbed, and then add the 'Knees to the ceiling' order before allowing them to move together. This might seem a somewhat long-winded process for what should be a perfectly simple movement between a free hip joint and a flexible ankle. Alas, many of us do not have these things. The hips are often fixed, one perhaps more than the other, encouraging a possible twist in the pelvis when the movement of the legs takes place. The ankles are frequently fixed and there is pressure down on to the arches so that the whole foot moves as the knees come together, or indeed move apart. Often the inner muscles of the thighs are wildly over-contracted and the knees want to 'pull' together instead of lightly moving together. Or in the very athletic types the legs might well be so overworked that the knees cannot come together at all, except by forcing them. With lots of knee direction when lying down, these tendencies can be avoided or gradually eliminated, so even in such an apparently trivial movement it is important to direct oneself properly.

The indirect approach

In so many of the improvements that we need and are working towards, the Indirect Approach is always the best – indirect in the sense that most of our attention should be on maintaining the guiding orders, not on the local adjustment, but also in the sense that many of these improvements cannot be brought about completely and immediately, but often require one area to improve before another can be sorted out. Thus the 'means whereby' have to be kept constantly in mind, rather than the 'end' to be gained. Also the indirect means of using a movement to encourage releasing is much more useful in bringing about real change, than merely repositioning ourselves in some rather mechanical way: in fact, always working to the principle of releasing out of problems instead of mechanically adjusting parts.

The shoulders too must be approached indirectly. You cannot do a great deal about them yourself at the start, except begin to notice how they get over-involved, so just try and leave them alone more. This in itself is very difficult and enough to occupy most of us much of the time. Without doubt the skilled manipulation of a teacher can help undo tense muscles in that area and encourage the shoulders to 'release and widen' and so become more integrated into the rest of the back, which probably needs to do much of the work which has been wrongly taking place in the shoulder area. With a good lower and middle back the shoulders have something to rest on when we are upright, but the shoulders need a good back of which to become part, particularly a good lower back; probably doing much of the work wrongly taking place in the shoulders and on which the shoulders can rest when we are upright. As ever, an improving back presupposes an improving neck-and-head relationship and so you must return to basics again. The neck, head, back and perhaps the front of the chest will need at least as much attention as the shoulders themselves when they are being considered.

When lying down, place the hands, palms down, on the front of the chest, tummy or on the hip-bones as this will help the shoulders to drop a little and spread perhaps; the placing of the hands on the floor or couch with the elbows away from the body, as the teacher will probably do, is an alignment that you will find difficult to achieve satisfactorily on your own in the early days in most cases, depending on the amount of tension in the shoulder girdle. If, or when, you can achieve this sort of alignment, the idea of 'each part releasing out of the nearest joint' is a useful one. It helps to prevent the common tendency to pull the arms into the shoulder joints, which often accompanies a tightened, narrowed, pulled-round, -back, -up or -down shoulder.

Think of the arm releasing out of a widening shoulder, with the front of the upper arm lengthening, as it is often contracted through over-work. Then think of coming apart either side of the crease in front of the elbow, to release the forearm. Similarly, think of the hand out of the wrist, especially releasing *under* (i.e. inner part) the wrist where we tend to tighten and shorten. The line of the forearm should continue more or less straight down into the thumb, with the fingers at a slight angle away from the body. This may feel a little odd at first, but happens quite naturally when there is freedom in the wrists and a good relationship of one part to another.

Imagine a rounded arch in the armpit to help prevent the armpit becoming pinched in with the upper arm tight to the body. Do not go around with your arms out like a penguin but neither pull them into the side. When using your arms as when lifting or carrying, think of the outer part of the upper arm doing more work. This does not necessarily feel very different, but it can help to spread the work-load in the upper arm so that it does not all go into overworked biceps which tend to pull the arm up into the shoulder joint and often fix the shoulder girdle. When the arms are placed on the floor in the way that the teacher positions them, you might notice that the wrists are not flat down on the floor or that one pokes up more than the other. If you try to force them down, then the shoulder will come up from the floor, rather like a see-saw. This is because of muscles being too contracted and, if one is higher than the other, then that side of the body is likely to be more shortened and the shoulder, in particular, more fixed. In time a greater symmetry returns and, as the shoulder comes undone, it widens, the inner part of the upper arm lengthens, the wrist releases and drops and the problem disappears. So once again do not 'end-gain' and try to force good results. Keep your attention on the indirect approach and means of changing. In time the shoulders will find their right level and become better integrated into the back. The line of the collar-bone might well change, the hollow 'salt-cellar' you often see on people is a good indication of over-tense shoulders and should disappear. It is a good idea to think of the line of the collar-bones being more or less parallel to the ground when you are standing, not up at an angle. The shoulder-blades might well drop a little too and should not stick out like wings nor be pulled in towards the spine but should lie flat against the rib cage very slightly at an angle as the rib cage is curved, but when you are lying down able to release and rest on the floor without being forced. The important idea to keep in mind is 'releasing and widening'. You cannot be sure where the shoulders will end up when they come undone but you can be sure it will be a better place than where they were beforehand.

Working on the floor like this is the best way of resting. If you are feeling tired, it is much better to put yourself down like this than to flop into an easy chair or curl up on a sofa, where you are almost certain to be collapsing, hunching, twisting and creating a great deal of pressure into the joints and distortion in the struc- ture. Even if you are too tired to give the right kind of attention to yourself and you drop off to sleep, it is better to do it in this position than in any other. Thus you are more likely to be in something akin to a reasonable state of 'balanced rest', making the relationing of one part of the body to another more reasonable, with more freedom in the neck muscles, with the head supported in a good alignment with the neck, the back muscles releasing into lengthened patterns, with the shoulders spreading, the legs in a good state of balance and the feet, toes and fingers releasing and lengthening, but not rigidly stretched.

You cannot overdo this basic releasing and sorting-out work on yourself. It should be part of the daily routine, and most people enjoy a good excuse to lie down regularly, so it is in no sense a chore. It is the best and most direct means of sorting oneself out and returning to a good neutral 'norm' of balanced rest. In time we tend to return to such a state between activities and movements whether standing, sitting or lying down, but in the early days we need positively to encourage it as often as possible. As modern living is usually so busy, so complicated and sophisticated, we can most of us frequently gain a great deal from lying down in this way and learning to STOP. We often have to do things to ourselves which are potentially harmful; work too hard and too long, sit all day, carry heavy loads or paint the ceiling, but if we have a reliable means of returning to a balanced state of rest such things do not matter so much.

Lying down is very useful in eliminating some of the build-up of tension that develops as the day progresses. Often we rush around because we have to, but then we go on rushing because we cannot stop, not because we need to. Not only does the body become over-active but the brain does too. Frequently we find ourselves chattering away internally to ourselves, carrying on an endless internal monologue to no great advantage. As you are lying down and ordering, it is as though you begin to control some of this chatter, harnessing it into something more useful and productive, linking up the brain with the body, encouraging and gaining harmony once more.

We are also gaining a better sense of our backs in this way, better than we can get in the upright position at this early stage when the back muscles will not be releasing easily and the spine will often be shortened or too curved. Here we have something – the surface on which we are lying – with which to gauge more accurately what the back is doing, and something over which we can let go and spread beneficially.

Most of us need to lie down for fifteen minutes or more to gain something really positive, but even the odd five minutes in the lunch hour can be useful, and we cannot do it too often or too much. Most of us need this opportunity to sort ourselves out regularly and frequently. It is a thoroughly practical way of dealing with all sorts of possible problems and situations that could wreck us. In a busy routine we need to come to rest frequently, to stop and deal with the perpetual motion machine that we seem to have become. Whilst sometimes not a great deal might seem to be happening in this procedure, what actually is going on is of such fundamental importance and benefit that it is imperative we do this work on a regular basis.

If you have done yourself some good by lying down, there is no point in ruining matters as you get up, so take care as you do this.

Getting up from lying down

• If you are on the floor, it is best to roll over to one side, perhaps allowing the knees to come together beforehand, having directed them appropriately, and bringing the arm furthest away from the side on to which you are rolling across the body to support yourself as you rise to a position in which you are resting seated on one buttock.

• Continue to get up slowly, on to both knees then on to one, then stand up as you bear in mind not to pull back the head but

Get up carefully by slowly rolling over to the side . . .

letting the top of it lead you, and thinking of the spine following, not hauling yourself up with the chin, shoulders or breast-bone raised.

● If you are getting up from a couch, you will end up seated on the side of the couch as you roll over, so you will need to hinge forward from the hip joints, keeping length up the spine and using the arms, but not hunching the shoulders to help yourself off.

● Similarly if you have a back problem and are in bed, rolling over to the side, as on the couch, to sit on the edge of the bed is probably the best way of getting up. Any other way of rising, say, sitting up in the opposite way to which you lay down, is more likely to make you lose anything you might have gained from lying down. You are more likely to lead with the chin, pull back the head, hunch the shoulders or pull up the breast-bone and have to overwork the abdominal muscles.

● By rolling over and rising slowly you are more likely to keep the freedom in the neck, the well-balanced head, the free shoulders, the extra length and width in the back, the greater freedom in the hips and buttocks, and so off you go to your next activity from a good, neutral state of rest and better starting point.

. . . using your hands to help yourself up

Part Two

The Intermediate Lessons

Working through movement

After a few lessons establishing the fundamental approach most teachers will begin to employ movements as a way of encouraging change and improvement as well as perhaps getting to grips with the individual's particular problems, but always emphasising the 'means whereby' matters can be changed for the better and the indirect approach rather than 'treating' specific problems at the expense of the whole. It is often within movement that we most strongly reinforce old harmful habits, and within new or complex activities and movements not only do we reinforce old bad habits but even add on yet another layer of mis-use on top of all the previous layers. If we are having difficulty in functioning in this area, usually through mis-use in the first place, we viciously add on a compensatory layer. Provided the old habitual way of moving has been inhibited and a new improved means through ordering has been allowed to take place, a new dynamic and dramatic degree of change can frequently occur. Of course, it will not always 'feel' better, easy or right; developing tone in the back and legs through good use can lead to a certain amount of healthy aching and temporary discomfort, especially if it is very different from what we have been doing in the past; but often it can feel noticeably better, lighter, easier, more efficient, and less effortful.

Applying the principle to any movement can be valuable though certain movements are more useful than others in encouraging improvement. The Alexander repertoire can seem rather limited, but certain basic movements are designed to bring about the greatest amount of change at a reasonable pace, and establish useful new patterns in the body as well as being something that we can apply in many activities. The good teacher will ring the changes and assess constantly the pupil's needs without boring him with constant repetition of some activities, though certain of these basic movements will initially require quite a lot of repetition in order to become a secure part of the pupil's experience and firmly allied to the improving sensory mechanism.

Working with a chair

Fairly early on in the course of lessons most teachers will use the movements of getting into and out of chairs in their work. It is a classic Alexander procedure in which F.M. himself wrought miracles of change and improvement on his pupils. It is a particularly useful movement as it is one we do dozens of times a day, usually badly. According to Alexander the chair is man's worst invention, in that it encourages such appalling habits, and those races who tend to squat on their haunches or sit cross-legged on the ground do not seem to suffer so much from arthritis in the hips or so many back problems as we who are spending hours of each day sitting in chairs. Most of us when sitting or rising bring into play a gross pattern of distortion in the musculature, with a huge amount of unnecessary effort and a total lack of connection throughout the structure with all this misplaced energy: in fact, sitting is a good way of exercising many of our worst habits. If the movement is performed well with suitable Alexander attention, an amazing economy of effort will be employed, encouraging length, lightness and a subtle flow and connection throughout the structure, which can be a vivid and valuable new experience to the pupil of how little he needs to do and of how much unnecessary interference he has been making in the past. Even if he feels insecure or off-balance he can still appreciate the 'ease' involved.

Getting into and out of a chair

Early on the teacher will have observed how the pupil tends to sit and stand and might well imitate him to show him in some detail just what he has been doing, and what bad habits he has been perpetuating dozens of times a day. More often than not the pupil will employ some pattern in which the alignment of the neck, head and back are radically interfered with. It is most common for people to start to sit by immediately over-involving the neck muscles and so prevent the head from being poised, well-balanced and playing the leading role, usually pulling it back and down, which not only interferes with the head but creates pressure down the spine. If they also tend to stick out the bottom as if to 'seek' the chair with it, this often has the effect of creating pressure up the spine, not to mention pulling the knees together and the legs up into the hip joints, so it is as though the spine is shortened from both ends. The neck and head might well be also pulled considerably down into the trunk, and the shoulders hunched up round the ears with the distinct possibility of some unnecessary involvement of the arms and a fixed chest. They therefore arrive on the chair in a shortened, collapsed, fixed and distorted heap, with the neck stiffened, the head interfered with, tense shoulders and a collapsed back. Arriving on the chair they might well then collapse further in the lower back, and if they are held up at all it is with tense shoulders. The whole ghastly business is then topped off by nine out of ten people crossing their knees.

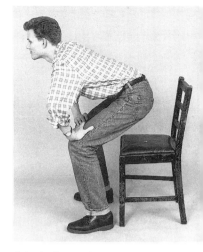

A typical mess!

Very similar patterns are reinforced when rising from a chair. As there is no tone in the back, and most people are starting off from a collapsed and distorted state, a further deterioration of this condition takes place just to get moving. Quite often people will start to move by leading with the chin, further stiffening the neck and pulling back the head, and because there is no follow-through from a supporting lengthened spine they will then have to push off with the hands, perhaps raising the shoulders and hurling themselves upwards with the front of the chest raised, the tummy thrown forwards and the buttocks clenched.

Not everyone does all of these things, but they are very common and most people will do some or most of them. Whilst it

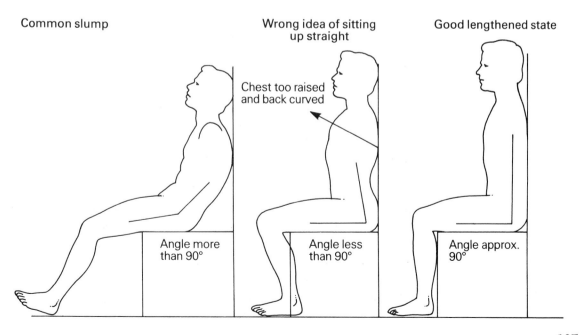

Common slump

Wrong idea of sitting up straight

Chest too raised and back curved

Good lengthened state

Angle more than 90°

Angle less than 90°

Angle approx. 90°

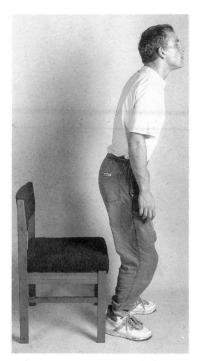

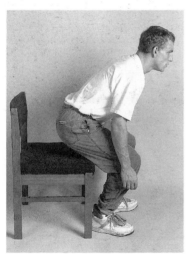

Examples of common misuse in sitting down and getting up

is not essential to get in and out of chairs 'properly' all the time, it is essential that we know what we are doing to ourselves in our habitual everyday activities if we wish to change our manner of use. Sometimes the opposite extremes can be equally harmful, those who have learned to move 'beautifully' or 'gracefully' – actresses, models, or dancers perhaps – who have been taught about 'poise', 'posture' and 'deportment' usually in the wrong ways. Often they will try to sit down or stand up in an over-straight way with the attendant strain and stiffness, not using the hip joints enough if the chair is low or the bottom is well back on it and 'forcing' the head up with yet another kind of stiffened neck. The wrong idea of 'sitting up straight' is as common as the wrong way of standing 'straight'. The breast-bone is forced up and there is a resulting loss of support and connection in the middle back just below the shoulder-blades. It is as though these people are sitting with a string pulling up the breast-bone, the knotted end of the string being just under the shoulder-blades in the back. The two extreme forms of mis-use when seated are sitting and then collapsing, as though arriving on the chair and then 'sitting again', and 'sitting up straight' in the wrongly conventional way in which many school children are taught. When seated it can be helpful to think of the angle of the thigh and hip-bone making approximately a right angle. If it is more than 90 degrees you are probably slumping; if it is less, then you are probably forcing yourself up. It will depend, to some extent, of course, on the length of leg and height of the chair too, and correct 'easy' lengthening will not always feel easy until a well-toned back has developed, by which time it actually hurts to collapse.

If we intend bringing about something better through these activities then obviously all these old habits must be inhibited and the feelings that go with them ignored. The last thing you should think about is getting your bottom on to or off the chair. The uppermost consideration should be the improved 'means', not the 'end' or 'result'.

Before sitting it is useful, but not essential, to have the feet apart, the toes slightly turned out at an angle of about 15 to 20 degrees if you are tall then rather further apart than if you are small.

• Stand in front of the chair with the backs of your legs just touching it, so as to be confident that it actually is there, but not bracing the knees backwards. With the feet further apart than usual you will be breaking up old habits – always a good idea in the early lessons – and then when the legs start to work they will do so in a better way.

• Whilst inhibiting the idea of moving, and then projecting the main guiding orders, the teacher will then with his hands check what you, the pupil, are doing in these areas and maybe coax slight adjustments, reminding you manually as well as verbally what you are inhibiting, and checking that your head is reasonably freely poised and that your back is not too interfered with to make the improved movement possible. The buttocks should not be too clenched, nor the chest and shoulders too fixed, nor the knees excessively braced. In fact inhibiting any preparatory tension.

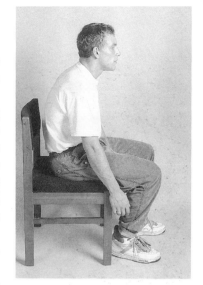

• It is a good idea to think of 'going up', always useful in a downward movement as it helps to prevent collapse, but 'thinking up' should not be associated with looking up, raising the eyes, or the front of the chest, and perhaps yet again pulling back the head.

• All you will have to do is bend the knees over the toes in the line of the foot, not over the arches or braced outwards past the line of the foot, as this is the way the legs are designed to work, taking care that you do not fix the hip joints and carry the pelvis forward, thereby missing the chair. Sometimes to indicate two points on a wall, two chairs placed apart or the two outside edges of a mirror if you are standing in front of one and observing what you are doing, is a useful way of giving you somewhere to 'aim' your knees.

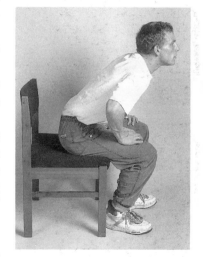

• Keeping the guiding orders uppermost in your attention, and, whilst still inhibiting any preconceived notions of how it should feel, you will then allow the movement to take place possibly on the instruction from the teacher to 'Put the knees away' or bend them, whilst the teacher is still guiding you with his hands, most likely attending to your head. If you have not lost your attention along the line and lapsed into old feelings, you should find yourself seated with a still-free neck, lightly balanced head, perhaps considerably lengthened in the back and with tone in your legs with the knees still apart.

This might well have felt odd or off-balance but it is quite likely it also felt easy, light and effortless. On arrival it is the length and width and good muscle tone in the back that should be supporting

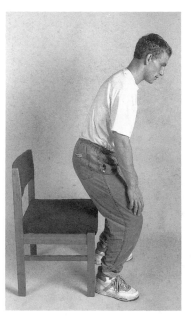

With careful attention one can maintain good alignment while sitting down . . .

you in an upright state, not a held chest, shoulders or stiffened neck. To encourage you to imagine your rib cage filling out into your back keeps the front of the chest free, and frequently gives an awareness of width to go with the length gained in the movement. The teacher can coax this into happening with his or her hands and often it is a relief to the pupil to free the chest in this way, though the back can feel oddly far back in space, but it should not be in the least collapsed or convexly arched.

Keeping an awareness of the neck, head and back the teacher might then deal with your arms and shoulders. The arms, provided they were not involved in the sitting movement, will be hanging at the side and the teacher will take them, one at a time, checking how 'fixed' they are, perhaps lifting them sideways and forwards and easing them out of the shoulder joints, carefully not disturbing you as you maintain your neck, head and back relationship. Thinking of the elbows dropping to the floor is often useful here as it helps to keep freedom in the shoulder joints and prevents the arms becoming rigid even if the teacher holds them straight out to the side or front. In general, thinking of parts dropping can cause undesirable collapsing, but in this case it can be useful, providing it does not encourage the shoulders to be pulled down. It is a good idea to place the backs of the hands, palms upwards and fingers uncurled, on the thigh fairly well up the leg, so that the weight of the arm is taken by the back of the hand, and there is less likelihood of the shoulders being pulled down, back or forward; it also allows for an easier freeing of the shoulders, and it is not a position which we often adopt, so it is less likely to be habitual. With the palms down there might be a tendency to grip the leg and reinforce habitual mis-use. The elbows should neither be pulled into nor held out from the side of the trunk – there is usually a middle place in most areas we are dealing with that is better than either extreme – and with reasonably flexible wrists and free shoulder joints.

The shoulders will then need attention and once again you will be encouraged to keep your main orders going but adding on the 'Shoulder release and widen' order as the teacher eases the shoulder out to the side away from the spine, widening front and back but with the appropriate emphasis for each individual, as you might be excessively pulling the shoulders back, or forward, up or down, as well as in. Keeping a sense of the back as the supporting area you will find that as the shoulders become free they gradually find their own correct level and become more integrated into the improving back.

The knees will also need to be included, the order is the same as when standing – 'forward and away'; in this case 'forward' so that they are not jammed back into the hip joint, and 'away' so that they are not pulled together. Even if the feet are less widely spaced and the knees are correspondingly nearer together they should not be PULLED together, nor should they be braced apart past the line of the foot, but directed out of the hips, forward over the feet. As with certain of the other orders we need both elements in the right sequence so as not to over-emphasise one at the expense of the other. If the knees are well-directed 'forward' it is difficult to brace them apart, and if they are directed 'away' they cannot be pulled together. Most people are not only collapsing in the lower back when seated but also pulling the legs into the hip joints and the knees together so that they are a great, fixed, heavy heap on the chair, whereas they should be lengthening upwards in the back, but not rigidly straight, and free in the hips with the legs in line with the feet, lightly perched on the ischial tuberosities, the two bottom points of the pelvis.

In many cases the heels will not easily be down on the floor without moving the feet forward. This depends to some extent on the height of the chair and the length of leg, but mostly it is because the ankles have become fixed and the muscles and tendons at the back of the lower leg have become shortened. This will sort itself out indirectly to some extent over a period, but 'insisting' on keeping the heels as low as possible is a good idea providing it is not too forced and becomes an end-gaining attitude at the expense of the attention to the other parts. Frequently one heel will be more raised than the other, indicating greater tension and mis-use on that side of the body.

When getting out of the chair a similar procedure should be employed.

. . . and arrive on the chair in a better state

- Inhibit the stimulus and do not worry about getting the bottom off the chair.
- Keeping the main guiding orders uppermost in your attention, the teacher will help maintain this direction with the hands and then, when you give consent to the movement, let your head lead, your spine follow, and allow your knees to move away over the toes without moving the feet. This will allow the legs to take

111

on the required tone and work, preventing them pulling back into the hips or together, but it must not be at the expense of the leading areas. The temptation is to think 'I must do something with my legs or get some leverage from down below somewhere' and this always prevents the right connection and flow in the movement with the various parts working in the proper order, especially the head leading. Nor do you need to push off with your hands and involve the shoulders or arms which should just hang freely as you let them go.

● If you have not 'lost' your head and have kept your back you should arrive in the standing position, reasonably straight with a still-free neck, a freely poised head, a properly lengthening and widening back with the buttocks and the chest quite free, and toned but not braced legs.

Again it might feel odd, but perhaps pleasantly so, with a realisation of how little effort is needed, how free of strain, lurching, hurling or pushing off the movement can be, and how your body feels free but connected with each part working in the right order.

As lessons progress a skilful teacher can bring about many improvements and useful adjustments when you are working in a chair, but there will need to be the constant attention to maintain or encourage a free neck, delicately balanced head and improved tone and freedom in the back muscles. An awareness of how the hip joints work by pivoting forwards and back is a good idea, making sure that there is no loss of length or connection in the back by bending in the spine. When pivoting back towards the back of the chair, be sure you do not brace your head back, or lose the support through length in the spine, collapsing in the lower back on arrival. When hinging forward do not let the breast-bone rise up or you will lose the follow-through of a lengthened spine and the head will not be leading. Also make sure you are not arching forward with a bent spine but really are using the hip joints. You can use such movements to gain some improvement on your own. If you feel, as you are seated, that you are collapsing, fixing, stiffening or aching, decide to move, inhibit the stimulus, give your orders and think of what they mean, then as you move forward, or back – more difficult – or even out of the chair, some improvement should take place; you can lengthen out of the collapse, release out of fixing, or ease out of the discomfort.

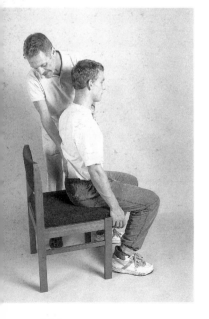

Using a chair for working with the pupil

Trying to get in and out of chairs 'correctly' in the early days is not such a good idea, as the teacher will almost certainly be giving you the guidance and confidence to make the movement more easily than you could do on your own. The teacher might well be taking you up and down straighter than you could possibly manage alone, just to give you a better and more vivid experience of what is possible, how little effort the movements really require, how economical they can be, how well-connected the structure can remain. So do not try to go too straight too soon, you will almost certainly panic, feel insecure or off-balance, and begin to fix the neck, chest and so on. You will shortly be made aware of how the hip joints should be used more and often need to be, if the chair is low, if you are rather tall, or if you want your bottom well back on the chair. There is no great virtue in sitting and rising in this very straight fashion, but as you progress you will in any case tend to become straighter as the legs develop more tone in connection with the improvement in the back, since they work together in this sort of movement.

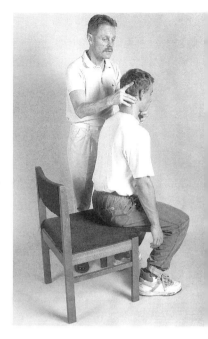

Sometimes when you are seated the teacher will place the feet further out from the chair, taking the leg at the knee so that the foot swings forward under its own weight and lands directly beneath the knee at a right angle to the thigh. This is often more comfortable for those with short legs or shortened muscles and tendons, or for most of us if we are sitting for a long time. As the great temptation is to help or shift the weight of the trunk back or sideways this must be inhibited, and the top part of the body maintained in its lengthened state. It can feel odd, but is a good experience of how we frequently shift our weight unnecessarily. It is better in this case to trust your orders, and your eye if you are sitting in front of a mirror, and not your feelings. Getting up from this position will also feel strange, difficult, or even impossible without resorting to some old way of hauling yourself out of the chair. It is quite simple but will 'feel' difficult as it goes against everything we have probably been doing most of our lives and all those feelings associated with the old habits. The teacher will need to hinge you more at the hip joint than if the feet were more directly under the body, but as you come forward be sure it is forward and UP and not forward and DOWN. Keep in mind the leading role of the head and the following lengthened spine at the crucial moment when the knees must be included to 'go away' over the toes. This way you can only rise; if you do not, you have

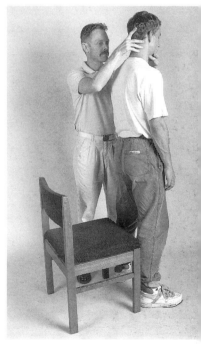

lost the sequence of attention, are resorting to old feelings, or are going forward and down and will land on your face. The danger point is when the knees come into the movement and we think 'Ah, now I must use my legs' and then forget everything else. Keeping a string of orders going becomes easier with practice until one is eventually giving the orders in the right sequence 'one after another but all at the same time'; and as in most activities where we might want to trust our old feelings too much it is vitally important to continue inhibiting the original stimulus right through the new 'means whereby'.

Sitting for long periods

When sitting for long periods it is a good idea in the early days to support the back in a lengthened state by using the back of the chair, as maintaining this state without support is not easy after a while, and it is all grist to the mill in developing a better back. In time this lengthened state will, however, become more and more comfortable and it will hurt to collapse. Even the worst-designed chairs usually offer some support, but in a deep easy chair you will probably need to put a cushion behind you. Get your bottom well back on the chair. If you need to shift it back, this movement too should be inhibited and attention paid to how you do it. In this case try to leave the shoulders alone but use the arms placed at your sides, elbows bent and the hands round the edge of the chair seat, or the knuckles down on the seat if it is wide enough, with the hand, wrist and forearm straight, not a collapsed forearm. By straightening the arm at the elbow you should be able to gain enough leverage to lift the bottom up off the seat and place it back, unless you have a particularly long back or very short arms. Be sure that you do not lift up the shoulders then the rest of the back, in two sections, but let the shoulder remain part of the back and lift the whole unit before placing it backwards. As you let the bottom down do not settle into yourself but try to leave the head up at the same height and so gain some extra length in the back. Even an apparently trivial movement like this can be useful if inhibited and then attended to properly. In this case you will perhaps have involved the shoulders less than usual and gained more of a back and a longer waist as well as maintaining a better neck and head relationship. Be sure that you are really using the back of the chair in the right way to maintain support, not relying on a held-up chest or shoulders nor pressing back into the chair, but lightly resting in a flexibly lengthened state. Placing the bottom forwards, either in a chair or on a couch, is a similar procedure, but be careful in this case not to 'scoop' the bottom forward and 'under' as you move it, but take the whole integrated top part of the body forwards and again only let the bottom down lightly.

Our worst enemy may be lifestyle. It is generally agreed that we sit too much and move around too little. We galvanise our generally unfit bodies into sudden strenuous activity (often in 'leisure' time). Our back muscles are feeble, floppy things compared to those of our grandparents, who had to walk to the shops, to carry wood and bend to light fires, to chop and beat and knead their food. Our inventive brains are likely to make physical activity redundant faster than our bodies evolve to cope with laziness.

Ismene Brown

Pupil easing himself back on the chair – without involving the shoulders

 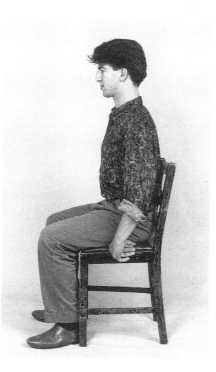 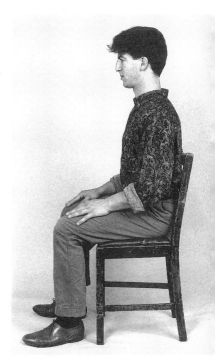

Working against a wall

Some pupils feel that their hip joints, knees and ankles do not flex easily when getting into and out of chairs and they are probably quite right, so some work to bring back tone to the legs and greater freedom in the joints is a good idea. Using a flat wall is useful here, and for other reasons.

Stand with the back to a wall but not leaning against it, the feet at least a foot apart, probably wider if you are tall as you will need a broader 'base'. The heels should be about two to three inches (five to seven centimetres) no more, away from the wall and the feet slightly turned out with an angle of approximately 30° between them. Check that your weight is evenly placed on both feet. A wall opposite a mirror is helpful but this is one area in which our feelings seem a little more reliable than usual. If the teacher is present he will be checking these things. Through projecting the guiding orders, make sure that you are not stiffening your neck unduly, that the head is reasonably well balanced, not pulled back, dropped forward, to the side, or the chin pulled in, in fact rather like a gas-filled balloon going up off the top of the spine. Keeping these in mind, next check the back, that you are not unnecessarily clenching the buttocks, swaying forward in the lower back, poking forward with the upper part of the spine from the 'hump', or holding up the breast-bone. Then keeping the top part of the body in mind, check the knees, that they are not excessively braced back or 'squinting' at each other.

Moving back to the wall

Decide then to pivot from the ankle back to the wall, but inhibit that idea and again keep the orders uppermost in your mind, so that you are considering HOW you are going to move. It is a good idea to think UP, as going back, like any downward movement, can be associated with tilting the chin up, pulling the head back, raising the front of the chest and creating pressure down the spine into the lower back. If you have started from a reasonable alignment, and have not lost it within this small backwards movement, the buttocks and shoulder-blades should hit the wall about the same time, but if you have a particularly large bottom or very clenched buttocks they might hit first, or if the lower back is thrown forward or the shoulder-blades very 'winged' or the sternum held up, it is likely that the shoulders will hit first. The

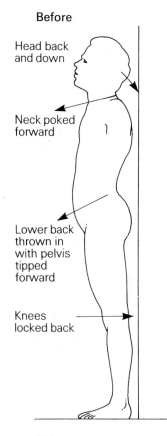

Before

Head back and down

Neck poked forward

Lower back thrown in with pelvis tipped forward

Knees locked back

head should not, in most cases, be touching the wall, or you are probably pulling back your head. If there is a twist in the chest or pelvis one side might hit the wall before the other. It does not matter much but is an interesting way of checking what you are doing to yourself. In any case the movement is designed to help you release out of such problems.

Going down the wall

Then give yourself the stimulus to move the knees away over the toes in the line of the foot, so that you slide down the wall. Again inhibit and order; do not stiffen your neck to bend your knees as so often happens. Think of going UP not down and, then, as the knees move 'forward and away', strictly speaking in a line between the big toe and the next, not over the arches or braced out past the line of the foot, you can use the movement to bring about certain improvements. If necessary you can release in the lower back, undoing the buttocks, so that the base of the spine moves further down the wall than the head. In fact you should be lengthening UP within yourself even though moving down in space. If you are working against a wall where you can observe yourself in a mirror it is interesting to see just how far you can move your knees away over the toes without your head moving down the wall at all. Unless you have an over-straightened lower back there is usually a considerable amount of extra length to be gained merely from releasing the buttocks and lower back muscles and allowing the base of the spine to move downwards. Even with an over-straightened spine there might well be room for considerable releasing, and with most of us there is often quite a bit of leg tucked up into the hip joint which can release out of it as we move. The head should be the last thing to move.

You can get used to moving your legs without interfering in the neck-and-head relationship. You can release the front of the chest if it is held, and often thereby gain a better sense of width in the back, a kind of fanning out of the back to the sides just under the shoulder-blades. You will certainly develop tone in the legs and make that important improvement in the connection of the legs to the lower back – two areas that should be well-toned and very supporting when in an upright position, able to do lots of work but of the right kind. As you are moving you are releasing into a better

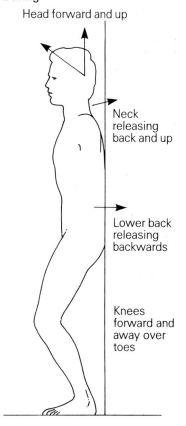

During

Head forward and up

Neck releasing back and up

Lower back releasing backwards

Knees forward and away over toes

state of balance as well as toning up the muscles; you cannot have proper tone without proper balance. The pelvis will have 'released under' as the lower back lengthens, and the tummy will have gently fallen into the back. Do not force the pelvis, tucking it under like dancers often do, but let it happen within the movement, releasing into it, not just mechanically repositioning it. Similarly with the tummy, if you are constantly pulling it in as opposed to gaining length in the back and allowing it to release back, you will only build up a great deal of extra tension there which can often be related to states of fear and anxiety.

Many of us are more contracted on one side of the trunk than the other, often with one hip more pulled up or one shoulder more pulled down. Your teacher might well have pointed out such problems, or you can begin to observe them in mirrors. Be aware of the likelihood and use this movement as a means of releasing out of such patterns.

Quite a lot can happen in this movement, but above all you should be gaining a good sense of your back from the wall, not forced back into it in a rigidly straightened way, but using it to assess extra length and width, and a definite improvement in the connection between the lower back and the legs.

Coming up the wall

As you come up the wall, keep all the things you gained when going down it. Let the head lead you up, not the breast-bone, which would probably make you lose the contact of the middle back with the wall. Do not raise the shoulders. Keep the knees over the toes, so that they do not pull together nor do you jam the legs back into the hip joints, but you maintain the improved tone. Stop frequently and check each area always in the correct sequence. Continue to move, keeping all these parts in mind, being extra careful towards the end of the movement when it is more difficult not to lose the new-found length in the lower back and clench the buttocks, tighten the chest or brace back the knees.

You should have gained a better connection throughout the structure when moving down the wall and maintained it coming up. Now you are going to use it to come away from the wall and this is probably most difficult of all.

Moving away from the wall

Do not push yourself off with the shoulders as you are liable to leave your bottom behind on the wall and to disconnect yourself in the middle or lower back and lose the extra length you have gained. Nor push off with the bottom as you might well leave the shoulders behind and likewise disconnect yourself. The head is the leading mechanism, so allow it to lead. Remember it is the head which governs this better total-pattern connection and more integrated state of balance which we have just been working on in this movement.

You will probably 'feel' that you have to push off but you do not; you need to use what you have just been encouraging: an improved connection throughout the structure. This is where pupils start to work out where the impetus for the movement comes from and where the 'work' must be. This is fatal, as in this mechanical approach the pupil inevitably loses the connection throughout the body and the direction of the whole structure and begins to trust his feelings. It feels difficult or even impossible without pushing off, so do not 'feel' but trust the orders. Keeping your main attention on the leading head, also think of leaving your back towards the wall but not leaving your bottom behind, stuck out, as you move. In fact you will have to 'allow' it to move away from the wall without pushing off from there, a subtle but important difference. It is a question of spreading the attention, most of it on the head but also including the back and bottom. If you keep your head as you do this, the right kind of work will occur in the legs and the ankles without you feeling that you need to do anything extra, and you should arrive slightly away from the wall. Remember that you are not trying to push off the wall, but to use the subtle but stable connection throughout the whole structure, and so you are not only moving away from the wall but are still maintaining the lengthening upwards force. Your weight should be over your heels, not thrown forwards on to the balls of the feet as often happens; your chest should not be raised nor collapsed; the buttocks should not have tightened, and the legs should be full of tone but not braced. You might well feel rather like an ape, perhaps slack or oddly insecure. Almost certainly you will not feel 'straight', even though you will probably be considerably straighter and in time taller than you are used to being, with much less strain and bracing of the structure, good tone in the legs, more

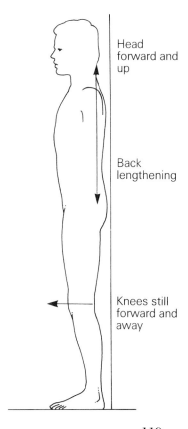

After

Head forward and up

Back lengthening

Knees still forward and away

119

length in the back, greater freedom in the chest and buttocks, and of course a nicely balanced head on a free neck, with the whole centre of gravity rather further back in most cases.

This 'back back' idea is often very useful to the pupil, and can become an extra order as the lower back improves. The only danger here is of over-straightening the lower back, which often goes with rigidity, and can be caused by 'tucking under' as dancers do with the pelvis. This is entirely different from using a movement as we are doing to bring about a releasing of the pelvis as the back lengthens, so that it takes up a better relationship to the rest of the back. Another possibility is that, as the lower back lengthens in the movement, there can be a compensatory poke forward from the 'hump' with the upper section of the spine, so sometimes the order 'Neck releasing back and up' can be useful.

This movement up and down a wall might seem like a perfectly simple exercise, rather like that suggested as a preparation for a skiing holiday, but it is not. First it should not be thought of as an exercise at all but as a movement which should be inhibited and ordered, so that a great deal can happen in this apparently trivial activity. You can release and lengthen out of any number of likely problems into a more symmetrical and better connected state throughout the whole structure, especially in the lower back and leg area, encouraging balance and tone, with extra freedom in the joints, a better placement of the work-load and an awareness of an improving back. It is a good way of getting used to using the legs without stiffening the neck or tightening the chest, as so often happens.

Having been taken through this movement carefully by the teacher several times, with a precise attention to all the details involved in encouraging improvement, the pupil can try to do it alone. However, you can slide up and down the wall for a month and you are unlikely to gain any kind of improvement, unless you are stopping the old reactions and patterns through inhibiting and encouraging new improved ways through ordering and the attention to yourself. If you do it, say, once a day for three or four minutes you should be inhibiting and ordering for at least ninety per cent of that time and only moving for the other ten per cent, so that the movement, when it is allowed to take place, is a manifestation of that attention, and not a reinforcement of old habits. Even if you only move a couple of inches down the wall something can improve. If the legs hurt when you do it, that is a good sign of mis-use, so do not overdo it. By doing it once a day with care and attention, and without forcing anything, you can be quietly revolutionised.

Rising to tiptoe

When you have become reasonably at ease in this movement and have developed more tone in the legs and a greater awareness of the back in a more lengthened and widened state, you can take it a stage further. The improvement gained by moving down the wall should be maintained when coming up, and can now be stabilised and strengthened by going further up the wall on to your toes. Be sure it is the head that is leading you up the wall, and not a raised breast-bone, which would probably mean you had lost some of your middle back; and follow through with the back in its better state: 'Use it, don't lose it'. Maintain this for half a minute or more and then decide to lower the heels, but only the heels. Be sure you do not sink down into yourself, each area settling down on to the one below, but keep a good sense of the back in its still lengthened state and maintain the overall force of levity – do not give in to gravity. It should be as though you are undoing down the backs of the legs to let *only* the heels drop. It was mainly in this area, the back of the ankles, where you shortened to go on to your toes in the first place, after all. Taking a great deal of care, and probably some considerable time, then come away from the wall as described above. At the end of all this you will possibly feel and probably be somewhat taller.

'Monkey'

The improvement in the legs and back by working against the wall will help with something known as 'monkey', something that should be applied in all sorts of situations and can be useful for all sorts of reasons. It is often a good idea to do this in front of a mirror in the earlier stages.

Once again stand with the feet apart and slightly turned out. Check yourself through the guiding orders and then decide simply to move the knees away over the toes in line with the foot, strictly speaking over the gap between the big toe and the next

Going into 'Monkey' by a) moving the knees away over toes and b) hinging at the hips, which move backwards, whilst maintaining length in the upper body

one, just like moving down the wall. I say 'simply', but even this apparently trivial movement is fraught with danger. It is common for new pupils to mis-use the hip joints and to take the pelvis forward towards the mirror, or to shorten the back and stick out the bottom, not to mention old ways of interfering with the neck and head or contracting, more down one side of the trunk than the other, perhaps displacing the chest over to one side, twisting round, or sticking out the hip. The use of a mirror will help the pupil here. It is as though the trunk is going down between two parallel lines, though again it is a good idea to think 'UP' as you go down as it is yet another chance to lengthen up within yourself even though you are going down in space – it will help you not to squash down into yourself. You can release the buttocks and allow the base of the spine to drop if necessary, likewise the front of the chest if it is too raised. It is always a good idea to use a movement to encourage releasing into a better state. Be careful not to over-tip the pelvis and pull it under, perhaps pulling in the tummy at the same time, but merely release into more length in the back, allowing the pelvis to keep or gain a better relationship to the rest of the back, as though encouraging a longer waist, otherwise you might well be bending low down in the spine and not simply using your hip joints.

Maintaining the guiding orders and the 'forward and away' direction to the knees, i.e., over the toes, let the hip joints travel backwards as you hinge in the hips. Again take care really to hinge here, as though the hip joints were low down and far back. Do not bend the spine, making it do what the hip joints should be doing – although flexible the spine is not a major joint like the hip. Do not stick out the bottom, so shortening the back. Be careful also not to bend at the 'hump'. It should not just be a mechanical tilt either, but a chance really to release and lengthen – a movement which can be used to ease out of twists or excessive curves. You should now be using the hip, knee and ankle joints at a half bend,

'Monkey' performed well

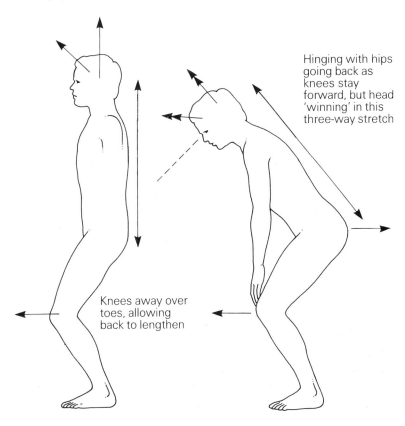

Hinging with hips going back as knees stay forward, but head 'winning' in this three-way stretch

Knees away over toes, allowing back to lengthen

123

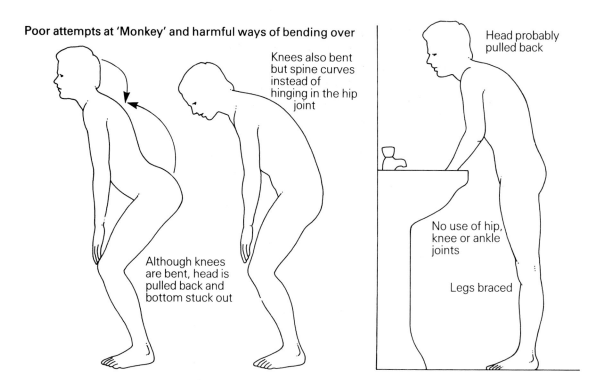

Poor attempts at 'Monkey' and harmful ways of bending over

Knees also bent but spine curves instead of hinging in the hip joint

Head probably pulled back

Although knees are bent, head is pulled back and bottom stuck out

No use of hip, knee or ankle joints

Legs braced

lengthening in all the parts between the joints, as opposed to shortening each part into each joint – as is so common. The knees should be well forward, the hips well back (a good thought to keep yourself steady without fixing), and the head as ever forward and up in relation to the top of the spine. It is like a three-way stretch, with the head just winning. If you have been working in front of a mirror your eye-line will of course have dropped as you hinged in the hip, otherwise you are likely to be pulling back your head. Do not pull back the head to meet the 'hump' or pull up the bottom to meet the 'hump'. In fact keep as much distance as possible between these three points without going to the opposite extremes of dropping the head forward and down or pulling the pelvis under. It is rather as though there is an arrow shooting up the spine into the skull, and another down to the base of the spine and two more shooting out of the hips over the toes. The arms should be left alone throughout all of this, just dropping under their own weight, but not pulling the shoulders down and round; rather you should keep going the idea of width across the front of the shoulders.

'Monkey' should be applied in many activities and usually needs to be practised quite a lot before it will feel comfortable, preferably with the teacher taking you through it several times before you attempt it on your own. In this movement the legs become well-toned, the spine lengthens more easily and the back is in a good state to take on any necessary work for lifting and suchlike; the shoulders can therefore do less work than they often habitually tend to do, and you will be using your joints properly. You can continue the movement down to the floor for picking something up, or apply it to anything for which you need to be at a low level, washing the hands, say, at a low wash basin, cleaning the teeth or writing on a table from a standing position. Rather than locking the knees back, excessively curving the spine and hunching the shoulders you can be 'exercising' good patterns. If you feel self-conscious in public, then put your feet nearer together and do a modified version of 'monkey'.

You can make the movement in two easy stages – a good idea early on to ensure that you keep all the necessary attention going to each part of the movement – or you can do it in one, letting the knees travel forward over the toes as the hips go back and you hinge in the hip joints, but it is not so easy to pay full attention to all the necessary areas involved when doing it this way. But with practice and care you will become more accomplished. When sitting down you will need to use it in this manner.

'Monkey' and sitting

If you want your bottom well back on a chair, if the chair is low or if you are tall, you will need to apply this 'continuous' monkey movement and use your hip joints properly when getting in and out of chairs. Once again be sure to maintain the main orders to the neck, head and back and not just think of using your legs. The good connection throughout the whole structure is most important and when a teacher is present he or she will be checking this and helping you to maintain it, but when you are on your own you have to keep it going through your own direction. Having inhibited the whole idea of sitting in the first place it is probably better not to think of it but to think of going 'up' and putting the knees 'away' as you hinge in the hip joints, continuing to move until you arrive on the chair without settling down. You will of course be at an angle, the trunk hinging forward, and will need to hinge back to the vertical. To do this you must still go 'forward and up', not letting the head pull back, and keep the length all the way up the spine. If you 'think' of coming back you might well collapse in the back, pull back the head, raise the breast-bone, create pressure down the spine into the lower back and hips. Any or all of the above are quite likely and very common. By maintaining the inhibitory factor and the neck, head and back direction, as you then hinge back to the vertical you should keep a nicely connected but not rigidly fixed neck, head and back relationship, using the hip joints freely and a good, lengthened back.

Similarly when getting out of a chair, the neck, head and back relationship must be kept as you hinge forward, and if you really are going 'forward and up' and then allowing the knees to go 'away' over the toes, you should rise without needing to push off anywhere. It is all very simple but not at all easy, as it goes against what most of us do most of the time, and it is fatal to think in terms of 'impetus', using certain muscles, or 'doing the work' some-

'Monkey' and sitting

While continuing the movement to sit, maintain 'directions', especially to head

Arriving in lengthened state

Continue 'forward and up' with lengthened back as you hinge back to vertical

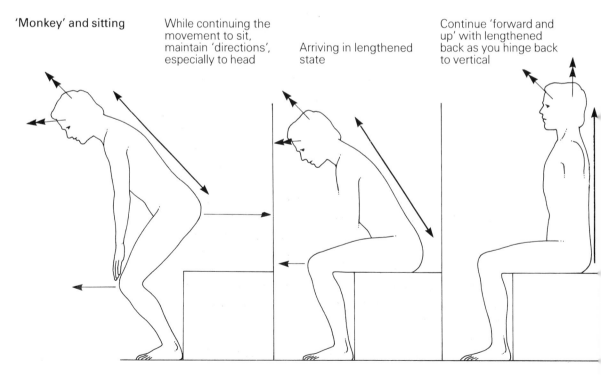

where. The work will be done in the right places to the right degree, particularly in the connection between the lower back and legs, provided you keep the general direction and attention going and do not lapse into 'feeling'. A new lightness, ease and economy of movement should emerge – a new, better 'feeling' in fact, and another good experience. Just be careful that you do not finish off the movement by leaving your bottom behind with buttocks clenched, or start to fix the front of your chest when you arrive at the standing position.

The feet do not necessarily have to be too far apart, and in public you might want them nearer together, but even here you can still apply the idea of using the hip, knee and ankle joints, keeping better length in the spine, and less involvement of the shoulders, often using a 'mini' monkey as it were, a less exaggerated version.

Getting used to leaving the shoulders alone and using the arms and hands in a better way is not easy but it is very important and you can help yourself by practising in the following way.

If you feel comfortable doing 'monkey' for several minutes without tiring and losing the detailed attention to yourself that this will require, you can work from this position, or you can try it from a sitting position with the feet and knees well apart. Although I use the word 'position' I do not like it, and I do not wish to suggest any kind of fixed state. Indeed, although steady and still in 'monkey' or seated, you should also be light, lengthened, delicately balanced and easily able to move freely from these places.

Place a fairly high-backed chair with a top cross piece that is straight or only slightly curved but reasonably flat and simple in front of you, the seat pointing away from you so that you are behind it. Sit yourself down or take up the 'monkey' stance carefully, bearing in mind the ideas of inhibition and projecting the main guiding orders. Then, whilst maintaining these, you will need to add on several others, so that you will be required to keep a long string of orders going throughout. This is not easy at first but becomes more so with practice.

When reasonably ordered, not only in the neck, head and back

Hands over the back of a chair

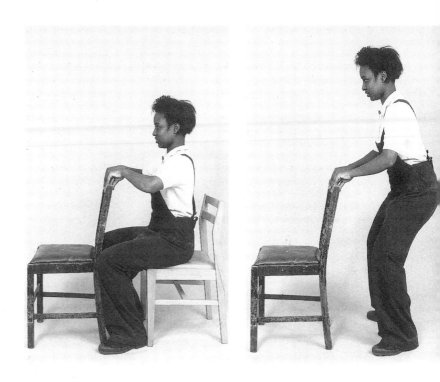

areas, but including the 'Knees forward and away' and 'Shoulders
release and widen', then decide to place one hand over the back of
the chair. Inhibit this movement, check the orders and then move
the hand so that the pads of the fingers and thumb are gently
gripping the chair rail, the fingers forward and thumb behind
nearest to you. The fingers should be straight and vertical, the top
of the hand from the knuckle horizontal, making a right angle with
the fingers. The wrist should be inwards and the elbow out, away
from the body with a slight pull to the elbow, the arm held out
more through tone and direction than through tension or fixing in
the joints. Think of widening the shoulders through into the front
of the upper arms. It often helps to think of the outer part of the
upper arm (triceps) doing a little more work than usual as this
often prevents the inner part (biceps) overworking as they usually
do and it brings a slightly better balance to the muscle pulls. This
is applicable to many activities involving the arms. Be sure you
are maintaining the neck, head and back, keeping a good sense of
support in the back, not collapsing and not beginning to curve
forward from the 'hump' and become drawn down to what you are

doing with the hand over the back of the chair. Attend to this frequently.

Next, decide to move the second arm, placing the hand similarly over the back of the chair alongside the first one, with a small gap between them – anything between a couple of inches (five centimetres) to about eight inches (twenty centimetres) is all right. It is often a good idea to initiate the movement in the arm from the elbow, taking it out to the side away from the trunk and then placing the hand. This helps to keep the width across the shoulders and prevents any interference in the shoulder girdle. You should now be ordering the neck, head, back, knees, shoulders, arms and hands – 'one after another but all at the same time,' as Alexander so often said.

With the hands in place imagine you are lifting up and gently stretching apart that piece of wood, the wrists in towards each other and the elbows, outwards. Try keeping the hands quite still, maintaining this 'lift and stretch', whilst releasing the shoulder joints and the wrists and moving the arms down and up again between a free shoulder joint and flexible wrist, rather like a chicken moving its wings. The idea is to keep up a generally well-ordered state as well as attending to the more particular area; keeping the connection throughout the whole structure, whilst

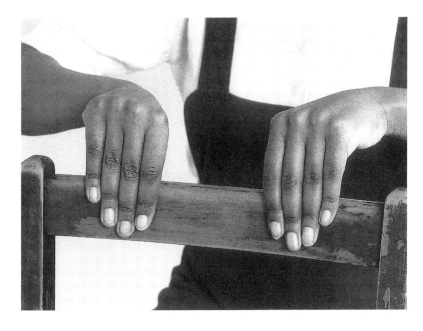

Think of lifting and stretching apart the piece of wood. Fingers should be straight, the top of the hands flat, the wrists in and the elbows out.

also developing greater control in the hands which can continue to work whilst you also move the arms without disturbing any other area. You can gain a better balance of the antagonistic muscle pulls around the wrists as you direct the wrists together, while keeping the elbows out, and more flexibility in the wrists as you move the arms. You will also experience how uninvolved the shoulders are and how free the arms can be whilst still doing something with your hands. Indeed you gain much more sensitivity, a far greater control and a much better feedback through the hands if you do not wreck everything en route to the hands, especially the neck, shoulders, arms and wrists. For an Alexander teacher, it is vitally important to gain this good use of the hands as they are constantly assessing what the pupils are doing and what they need through this means, but it is applicable to many activities for us all, very obviously to playing musical instruments, painting, typing, writing, washing dishes, or handling delicate objects.

If you become tired, stop, remove the hands, perhaps placing them with the backs down on the thigh if you are sitting, but be careful not to lose the width in the shoulders or collapse generally. Then, keeping your length, rise to an upright position if you have been in 'monkey' or hinge back to a comfortable place if seated.

Part Three

Later Lessons

Breathing

One of the marks of a good teacher of the Technique is, according to F.M., being able indirectly to induce good breathing, or at least an improvement in this area. You cannot impose good breathing patterns on to a faulty mechanism so, as in all our work, the approach should be through the 'indirect' means. Sort out, free up, and co-ordinate the mechanism and the breathing will automatically improve.

There comes a time during the lessons, however, when it becomes helpful to include breathing specifically in our attention, providing the general co-ordination is improving and this total-pattern improvement can be kept in mind. As it takes some considerable time with some pupils to get to this stage, but less with others, this opportune moment will vary tremendously as to when it presents itself. This indirect approach makes nonsense of those books that tell you how to breathe 'correctly', without encouraging improvement in many other areas, or merely try to teach you good breathing exercises. Good breathing should be the automatic norm if the circumstances are right, but they rarely are. So, once again, more attention and work are needed on the means than on the end.

Breathing is most efficient, with the greatest movement of the rib cage sideways and of the diaphragm up and down, when we are in the upright position, provided the balance, alignment and use of the body are good. But as this highly sophisticated and subtle state is sadly lacking in most of us, breathing will often be more efficient when lying down. One good reason for doctors telling us to go to bed when we are ill is because we more easily lapse into poor use when we are ailing, with even more tension, collapse or depression than usual, and thereby prevent efficient breathing, so going to bed will at least probably allow the patient to breathe better.

Certain general rules are useful when considering breathing. First, 'Don't forget to breathe'. It is amazing how many people hold their breath when making any kind of effort or when 'concentrating', immediately exacerbating their problems; they then wonder why things seem so difficult. In activities like climbing stairs or hills, just remember to keep on breathing, not by feeling you have got to make some extra effort but simply by not holding your breath. It is also useful to remember the opposite extreme, when you might be doing very little, as when reading or studying, and you might well be breathing too shallowly. Secondly, breathing should be largely a back activity, not too high in the front of the chest as is most common. So fly to your back with your attention when you feel you might be holding your breath. Thirdly, good breathing depends on a free but well-coordinated structure, with the rib cage moving easily sideways, and with good support from a well-toned back which allows for the natural support needed in the abdominal muscles. The front of the chest should not rise up nor the tummy muscles be over-involved. Look at a young healthy child before it has acquired a lot of bad habits, asleep in a cot, and you will see that the movement sideways of the rib cage is almost all that is necessary. The largest part of the lungs is low down, surrounded by the more mobile lower ribs: the floating ribs at the back and those unattached to the sternum (the breast-bone) in front, which are linked together only with the cartilage of the costal arch, supported at the base by the diaphragm. Here is where you should sense the greatest movement, NOT the sternum rising up, as happens when you are told to 'take a deep breath, chest out, shoulders back', with probably the shoulders rising too. You cannot gain the fullest intake of air this way. In fact you positively interfere with the lungs working to their fullest capacity, and with the working of the inter-costal muscles (the muscles between the ribs), which should allow the rib cage to move outwards.

The diaphragm is a large, pancake-like muscle across the base of the lungs. It is at an angle, slightly higher in front than at the back. There are major nerves from the neck to the diaphragm – the phrenic nerves – the sole motor nerves to the diaphragm, as well as direct connective tissue; so once again we have to go back to the basic idea of keeping a free neck in order for the other parts to function properly. The rib cage, roughly conical in shape, should expand sideways as the air goes in, and the diaphragm should descend and flatten out. As you breathe out the diaphragm will rise upwards, somewhat dome-like, and the inter-costal muscles will also release, allowing the rib cage to move in again. If the sternum has wrongly risen when breathing in then it should drop again when breathing out. Usually exhaling takes two or three times as long as inhaling depending on what you are doing. Air is pulled in on a vacuum principle, there is no need to 'suck'.

The back should be lively, strong and very supporting with the spine lengthening in a flexible manner and the abdomen a naturally-toned corset of muscle. It should not be held in and over-tight, as happens when we have a fear of developing a pot belly. This will create excessive tension which can often be associated with fear and anxiety. As the back improves and takes on more work, so the tummy muscles can release, before gradually building up the correct amount of tone in conjunction with the back, and become properly supporting without being over-tense. The major organs in this area will be able to function most efficiently, as they will be correctly supported, and with a natural internal massage from the freely-moving diaphragm. If the back is rigidly straightened and the tummy over-tightened, the major organs will be held in a kind of vice with consequent interference in their functioning. At the opposite and more common extreme, if the back is thrown in with an excessive curve in the lumbar spine, or collapsed with the tummy too slack and poking forward with a tilted pelvis, then all the major organs will be considerably displaced and unsupported, with a disastrous drag factor on the diaphragm. This can be a definite contributory element to certain ailments, and may even be the cause. So we do not want a state of collapse or flaccidity in the muscles, nor do we want a constricting band of tension around the middle, but a nicely-toned corset of muscle which supports us in a well-balanced alignment, allowing for better breathing to take place.

Start to notice how you are breathing. Get yourself well-ordered and reasonably sorted out, either standing, sitting or, in the early stages, preferably lying down as I've already described. You could try placing the backs of your fingers on your sides by the lower ribs, the hand curved with the wrists down, away from the shoulders, trying not to disturb the shoulders as you do this. It gives you something to focus on as you think of widening and a way of sensing the movement. You should notice a sideways excursion of the ribs. Try to maintain a steady, but fairly slow rhythm, remembering that breathing out usually takes considerably longer than breathing in. Think of something calming like a cat asleep in front of a fire or waves gently moving forward and back on a beach. The movement should be smooth and flowing, with no fixing at either extreme of widening to breathe in or releasing to breathe out. Check that the sternum does not rise as you inhale, nor should the tummy be pushed out, though as you

Good breathing

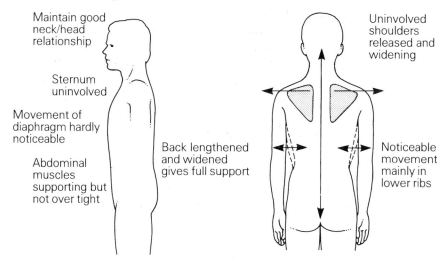

Maintain good neck/head relationship

Sternum uninvolved

Movement of diaphragm hardly noticeable

Abdominal muscles supporting but not over tight

Back lengthened and widened gives full support

Uninvolved shoulders released and widening

Noticeable movement mainly in lower ribs

Good alignment vital

exhale you should feel a slight tightening of the tummy muscles at the end of the movement; you will therefore need to release them as you let the back widen once again for breathing in. Breathing out requires more attention than breathing in. We often do not breathe out fully, merely exhaling about half a litre of the four or so litres of air in the lungs. If you breathe out fully, breathing in has got to happen without you needing to do anything. The air will go in of its own accord; there is no necessity to suck in the breath if the structure is reasonably free.

Once you have established this rhythm, and yet still keeping your mind on the general orders, try counting, aloud, fairly slowly up to ten or more as you breathe out, without altering the rhythm. Do not make any preparatory tension for the sound by raising the breast-bone or fixing somewhere in readiness; nor, as you count, should the activity become jerky, clenching, twitching, or snatching extra breath in the diaphragm, tummy or breast-bone. So often when you ask a pupil to speak loudly or count in this way, they feel the need to take in extra breath, and do so by raising the breast-bone or snatching in the diaphragm in preparation. This only makes things worse, as in doing these sorts of things they have instantly lost the freedom in the rib cage and the width in the back where most of their breath should come from. It merely reinforces their false sense of security. If the movement is free but properly controlled and the rhythm gentle and even, there will be lots of air in the lungs to cope with this simple counting procedure. In through the nose and out through the mouth is a good idea. You then use the natural filter mechanism in the nostrils, and it is more difficult to tighten the throat or vocal mechanism as you speak. If you lose the smooth flow as you make the sound, or run out of breath before you have reached 'ten', you are probably not properly prepared and no amount of trying to get it right will help, until you go back to sorting yourself out generally – only then can the whole process be properly effortless. As in so many areas the new, easier way of breathing can feel quite strange if you have been used to breathing wrongly for many years. It can feel quite alarming to someone who has been breathing incorrectly for years to allow the natural process to re-establish itself. Often, when a pupil is in a good state where the whole psycho-physical mechanism is well-ordered and suitably free, he or she will almost feel as though some external force is doing the work and that one is being 'breathed'. As is often the case, what is happening will be something much simpler than before and yet it might well feel less easy until the new patterns have become properly established and the 'norm'.

Until recently many voice teachers taught something called 'rib-reserve breathing'. Its basic principle was that the actor or pupil learned first of all to widen the back to breathe in, and then used only the diaphragm to breathe for shorter lines of dialogue, but, when a really long line arose, in which it was inappropriate to take a breath, there was lots of breath in reserve to deal with this line. Unfortunately, this led to a forcing-down of the diaphragm in most cases, and a rather unpleasant 'pregnant' sort of bulge building up under the costal arch, below the sternum, as well as too much fixing of the rib cage in its widened state, as opposed to the much more common fixing in the narrowed state. Rather surprisingly, this method of breathing helped to develop many good voices in the theatre, but from my own experience I would suggest it was only through the rather fortunate accidental effect of actors and singers actually realising that the rib cage COULD expand sideways and that breathing is mainly in the back. Once the performer was on stage he or she was so busy getting on with the business in hand that he forgot about 'correct breathing' and, through having learned to widen it, tended to be better, as a

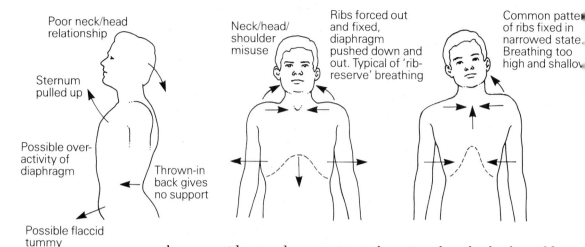

Poor neck/head relationship

Sternum pulled up

Possible over-activity of diaphragm

Thrown-in back gives no support

Possible flaccid tummy

Neck/head/shoulder misuse

Ribs forced out and fixed, diaphragm pushed down and out. Typical of 'rib-reserve' breathing

Common pattern of ribs fixed in narrowed state. Breathing too high and shallow

happy accident and a security in knowing that the back could work. Whilst actors and singers have to learn to control their breathing more accurately than most people, you cannot do more than breathe to your fullest capacity in a free but controlled manner and no amount of forcing the ribs out or diaphragm down will do any good, especially as this sort of thing cannot easily be maintained and will quickly be forgotten and lost in a difficult situation like performing. Fortunately 'rib-reserve breathing' is rarely taught now, and there is much more emphasis on encouraging the more natural, efficient and less erratic way of breathing, through the more precise but indirect means of re-educating the whole mechanism to function more reasonably. We are asking for something much more subtle and complex but much more natural, not a crude forcing of one area with no consideration of the whole.

Whispered 'Ah'

When you are progressing well in your lessons and you are able to maintain control of a freer structure, your teacher will probably suggest you try a whispered 'ah' sound. In this activity it is essential that you be able to maintain a long series of orders to yourself, so for most pupils it is pointless to try to do it too early in the course of lessons, as it usually takes some time for most of us to be able to keep this kind of attention on ourselves through even the simplest of activities.

You can try this, sitting, standing or lying down, though probably the latter is best in the early days, as you will be able to maintain a reasonable state of balanced rest more easily whilst releasing into a fair state of coordination. After a while, working in front of a mirror will be useful too; you can then observe exactly what the jaw and the tongue are doing.

Sort yourself out, ordering in particular the neck, head and back, then include the legs and shoulders in your attention. Then, keeping all these areas in mind, give some thought to correct breathing, inhibiting any old faulty habits of which you should by now be aware. Then decide to open your mouth. Inhibit this idea and give your basic orders once again. Frequently when one asks pupils to do this, they immediately disturb the balance of the head by either pulling it back or pulling the chin down and the jaw into the neck. Think of the jaw as very separate from the main body of the skull – it is this main section that you are ordering 'forward and up'. There is a large input into the nervous system in the jaw area, and unnecessary tension can be disastrous. I'm told that back pain can be caused thus. Jaws come in many states, shapes and sizes. There is the pushed forward, over-shot jaw, or the retracted, pulled-in variety: both maintained by too much tension. Such possibilities will need to be borne in mind in this activity, and the appropriate sort of releasing encouraged.

The jaw articulates between two points in front of the ear: when it is closed, at a near point close to the centre of the front of the ear; and then, as it opens, moving down and forward a little in an arc to the other point. You should be able to feel a hollow just in front of the ear below the centre point as the jaw moves. If you habitually pull the jaw in or tip the head back to open your mouth, when you inhibit these patterns the jaw might feel oddly forward as it moves. A jaw that is either jammed shut, or over-relaxed, very slackly open as with the old-fashioned village idiot figure, is quite undesirable. It should hardly ever be in either extreme state, though many people grind their teeth and clench the jaw much of the time and we often need to aim for the more released state. When vomiting the jaw is usually nicely forward and free, though I doubt if we appreciate it at the time. It helps to release the facial muscles if you think of something amusing, as though you are just about to smile, as you open the mouth. When you have mastered this use of the jaw, it should be practised so that it begins to feel familiar and in time correct.

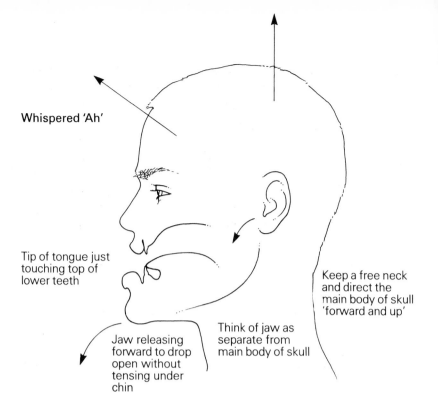

Whispered 'Ah'

Tip of tongue just touching top of lower teeth

Keep a free neck and direct the main body of skull 'forward and up'

Jaw releasing forward to drop open without tensing under chin

Think of jaw as separate from main body of skull

Notice what your tongue is doing. There is frequently a lot of tension in the use of the tongue and not enough control. Is it clinging to the roof of the mouth or narrowed in some way? Let it spread and lie flat rather like a shallow spoon with the tip of the tongue just touching the top of the lower teeth. Think of a nicely open throat so the back of the tongue should not be raised. Keeping all these things in mind – neck, head, back, knees, shoulders, chest, breathing rhythm, a hint of a smile, and tongue – allow the jaw to release well forward to drop open in an arc, but do not tighten under the chin and pull it into the neck; then allow a whispered 'ah' sound to escape. Don't force it. It should be like escaping gas. Don't 'voice' the sound but just whisper it as you breathe out. Don't let it happen until you are sure you are ready. If in doubt go back and check your orders. We usually need to give more time to this than we realise. The sound should be the final result of a great deal of preparation and will indicate how well you have attended to this.

If the sound is jerky, squeaky, wheezy, staccato, strangulated into an 'ugh', neutralised into an 'ur', spread into an 'eh', or anything but a pure, full but devoiced 'ah', something is amiss. Think of the sound being 'round', the mouth also rather recklessly so, open wide enough to pop in a plum, and the throat well open. If the tongue is flat and the throat open, you should notice a cool rush of air right to the back of the tongue when you breathe in through the mouth. To improve the sound and make sure it is not being pushed out, it seems to help to think of it coming out between the eyes or the centre of the forehead: it encouraged it to be well forward and free without being forced.

Do not try it on every breath unless you are certain that you are maintaining a long string of orders or sequence of attention, but a half-dozen whispered 'ahs' works wonders. It is useful in cases of sea-sickness or queasiness. It prevents tension associated with shallow breathing, and seems to help change the stale air at the bottom of the lungs which does not get shifted often enough, and it is excellent for hangovers! It gets more oxygen into the blood stream, so you might well want to yawn or laugh as you release into it. You should practise so that a free jaw does not feel so oddly forward, and even when it is closed the teeth should be barely touching, not jammed together, nor with the lower teeth shoved up behind the top teeth, though this will depend to some extent on your bite.

This is excellent basic sorting-out work, requiring detailed and subtle attention to yourself in several areas at once, but the more you try it the quicker you seem to get back to a reasonable state of controlled freedom, maintaining a better use of the breathing and vocal mechanisms.

For people who use their voices professionally there is no better way of preparing for their work. Once this basic activity has been mastered you can then go on to try other sounds, but an 'ah' is the purest uninterrupted sound you can make. For the stutterer or stammerer it is essential to work in this detailed way and should prove to be invaluable, but it will take some considerable time to achieve lasting results with most pupils. The problem in such cases is that all their security is in very strong old habits, tension patterns and often over-quick but frustratingly inappropriate reactions. These reactions need to be gradually replaced with a much better general coordination and re-educated sensory mechanism related to the much subtler, freer but better controlled new state. Most people stutter in some area or other; it is just unfortunate that those who do it with the speech organs, the most obvious area of communication, are the most noticeable.

Standing

Whilst most pupils will have been attending to themselves in all sorts of ways from quite early on in the series of lessons, in the first stages this will have been rather crude (Re-read 'Attending to oneself' on page 73), but after a while it should become less so. When you have experienced much of the Alexander repertoire a number of times you should be able to monitor what you are doing more reliably, at the very least you should begin to know when things are wrong, even if you are not too sure when they are better – there being no such thing as 'right' as a rule.

Keep checking your general alignment when standing in those odd moments when you've nothing else to do.

- Go through the orders – neck, head, and back.
- Make sure you are not shortening the spine by clenching the buttocks. Or holding on to the upper part of the front of the chest.
- Or throwing your back in any more than you can help. By this time you should be doing these things less and the back should be noticeably improving.
- Also check your knees: order them 'forward and away' if necessary; then, with most people it is a good idea to take yourself back, often fractionally, from the ankles whilst still lengthening upwards in the back – i.e. 'back and up' – to make sure that the weight is not thrown forward over the balls of the feet but is evenly placed over the heels, slightly to the front of the heel to be exact. It should not be pressure downwards, but just the point of most direct contact. The back should now be well lengthened, but not rigidly over-straightened, and with most people further back in space – considerably so in the case of those with a pronounced lower back curvature.
- Be sure when checking this that you do not poke forward from the 'hump' when trying to get the back back. 'Up off hump' as well as 'Back well back' are good orders for many of us.

By releasing the buttocks you will not get a saggy, slack bottom, the thing most feared by beauty magazines. Indeed, by releasing the buttocks IN ORDER TO lengthen the back, in conjunction with the 'Knees forward and away' direction, you will develop tone in this area. A clenched bottom can cause havoc in the way of urinary and sexual functioning, and in other major organs in this region.

Sometimes I liken this improvement to playing with children's building blocks. If you place them exactly on top of each other you can go on upwards for a long time, but if one is slightly askew, off-centre, you have to make a compensatory adjustment and the whole structure becomes insecure and soon topples over. It is rather the same with the body, each part needing to be stacked precisely above the one below. If it is not, there will be harmful, unnecessary pressure into the joints and an over-contraction of the muscles between the joints. There will also be, as a consequence, interference in the natural lubricating mechanisms in

Encouraging balance

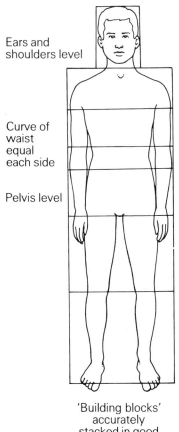

Ears and shoulders level

Curve of waist equal each side

Pelvis level

'Building blocks' accurately stacked in good symmetrical stance

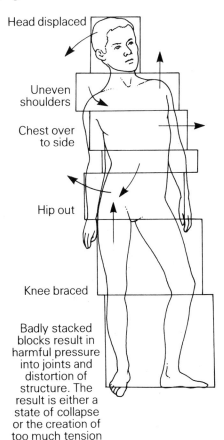

Head displaced

Uneven shoulders

Chest over to side

Hip out

Knee braced

Badly stacked blocks result in harmful pressure into joints and distortion of structure. The result is either a state of collapse or the creation of too much tension in order to remain upright

Easy symmetry

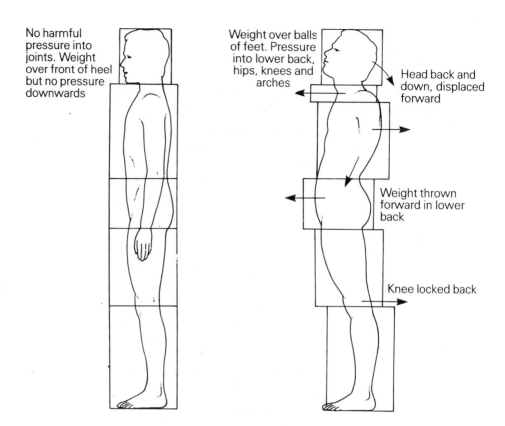

No harmful pressure into joints. Weight over front of heel but no pressure downwards

Weight over balls of feet. Pressure into lower back, hips, knees and arches

Head back and down, displaced forward

Weight thrown forward in lower back

Knee locked back

those joints and the beginnings of arthritis and all sorts of painful ailments, not to mention a reliance on harmful tension patterns instead of the much more desirable awareness of subtle stability and lightness. The upright stance is often blamed for many of our problems, and obviously four points of contact with the ground are more stable than two, but not so practical when needing to move or react quickly or when looking about us. Being upright is more useful to us in a civilised world, but being much more subtle and delicate it can easily go wrong, and usually does.

But by now the balance and alignment of the body should be changing, and improving with consequently less wear and tear on the structure, maintaining the 'force of levity', less pressure into the joints, more tone in the supporting muscles, less unnecessary involvement of specific, secondary muscles and an improvement in how the weight is distributed.

Walking

It is too difficult to sort out walking problems very directly in the early days and more important to work on a programme of general re-education and improved coordination in all areas. As this continues, however, you should find it indirectly but advantageously affecting your way of walking.

Certain general rules must be kept in mind when you begin to think about this area. First of all it is essential to keep the main guiding orders going throughout the activity. In fact it is a good idea to get used to ordering when walking as it then does not become associated in your mind merely with stillness or preparing to move but is linked to actual movement itself and a state of fluidity. By now these orders should mean quite a lot to you and be associated with numerous areas of improvement; a better back for instance with pelvis integrated into the back, stable yet free.

As the lower vertebrae become unlocked and the muscles in the lower back lengthen – something that needs to happen with many of us – so it becomes easier to keep length in this area, and for it to become stable and connecting.

When picking up the foot, the tendency is often to shift the weight excessively over to the opposite side, and then, as it is placed down in front, for the weight to be thrown back again as the other foot comes up. These shifts of weight cause tremendous unnecessary pressure downwards into the hips, knees, ankles and feet and so they should be minimised by keeping the general length in the structure. There is a definite lengthening force upwards when the neck muscles are free and in a state of balance, allowing the freely poised head to be dynamically leading and the muscles supporting the vertebral column well educated into a lengthened state. This 'force of levity' counteracts the force of gravity quite adequately but, unfortunately, most people have no conscious experience of this. Most little children have it instinctively and naturally. When they are running around and suddenly sit down abruptly on the floor they do not jar their spine, nor is the poise and balance of the head – much heavier in relation to the body than in an adult – interfered with.

Walk behind people in the street and notice just how much effort goes into throwing the weight from side to side and pulling down in the body, maybe hunching up on one side, and pulling

Carrying shopping frequently encourages all sorts of distortion

over to the other, very common in those who carry shoulder-bags. It is amazing how some people propel themselves forward at all: so much effort do they make to go in other directions.

It is usually a good idea to think of the lower back going back to where you have come from, but with the bottom not sticking out. The lower back is usually further back in space as the back lengthens, and the centre of gravity in a better place. This can feel odd if you are used to going forward with a shortened spine, held chest or pelvis thrown forward.

As you take a step, the side of the pelvis should not be pulled up but you should be using your hip joints and moving from there. The pelvis and lower back should not be destabilised. It is as though the knee initiates the movement, raising it and going on to the ball of the foot, picking up the foot; then the whole body will incline forward slightly, and it is then that it is important to keep on lengthening – in fact think 'up' as you then put your foot down, the heel touching slightly ahead of the toe.

Try the following in a fairly large room with a full-length mirror, if you get the chance. Stand at the opposite end of the room from the mirror on which you have placed a small mark, say a blob of lipstick, at a point opposite the middle of your forehead or directly above the top of your head. Position yourself at the opposite end of the room directly opposite or under the mark. Try walking towards the mirror keeping the mark in the same place. You will probably find that it seems impossible as you will almost certainly be swaying from side to side. Some people will insist that there has to be a slight weight shift but I have seen it to be quite imperceptible in those whose use is really excellent. The main point is to try to minimise this unnecessary weight shift and harmful downward pressure. Get yourself well-ordered and, keeping in mind all the above ideas, try again with smaller steps. Start the movement in the knee and continue to go 'up' as you put the foot down, and so on with each step. Keeping your main attention in the head often helps, as does varying the pace sometimes. To work things out carefully you will need to slow down and take shorter steps, but sometimes to get well-ordered and then walk quickly prevents you getting bogged down in the old feelings and you can keep the central line more easily. Walking backwards away from the mirror is sometimes easier on this straight line, as we do not usually have such strong habits or definite feelings in this less familiar activity.

Work programme

If you are keen you will be working on yourself in all sorts of ways after a couple of dozen lessons, or even fewer. You might well find certain improvements happening indirectly in any case, even when not thinking specifically about the Technique, and some of them will have been absorbed and will have become part of the by-now improved, more familiar, new pattern. After all, the improvement is only re-establishing what should have been there if circumstances had been ideal – which they rarely are – so when the change finally occurs it is often quickly absorbed, even to the extent that you will sometimes look back and wonder what the fuss was all about; but if the teacher could put pupils back into the state in which they were when they started lessons they would probably be horrified, just as at the commencement of lessons if the teacher could by magic propel pupils forward by a couple of dozen sessions they would not like that either. Now and then you can remember back. Sometimes I work on a pupil with a particular problem and I think 'I bet I was just like this before I started', but usually it is difficult to appreciate how gross, clumsy, misused and badly coordinated one used to be.

Nothing takes place in the lessons that is not part of the natural process and, *if you allow it to happen*, in time a great deal of the work will be done for you. However, you have to give it a chance and this is where working on yourself comes in.

Apart from the Alexander awareness of oneself that tends to hover constantly at the edge of one's general attention, and the already-absorbed improvement, work can be thought of as the pure kind and the applied sort, but you cannot apply the principle until you are well-versed in the pure work. This happens initially in the lessons but, after a time, you should be setting aside, as part of the daily routine, certain periods for pure work on yourself. Indeed, working on yourself is, eventually, much more important than having lessons; this is the REAL work. Now and then, however, there might be the odd occasion, period of despair, or emotional crisis when working through it might seem too difficult, perhaps desperately wanting some temporary relief or maybe losing patience with the idea, and here a teacher can be a great help, encouraging you back to a more receptive state in which work can once again begin.

When lifting, don't put all the strain in the shoulders and back

In the area of pure work the lying-down sessions will always be valuable, especially for those leading a busy life. Using a mirror is useful for observing oneself when working in a chair or perhaps doing some pure 'monkey' so that it begins to feel comfortable and secure. Working against a wall is invaluable, especially in the early days, to familiarise yourself with a better back and gain more tone in the legs in connection with this improved back, with the consequent change in the balanced alignment. The 'Whispered "ah"' reminds you to keep the *general* attention going during a *specific* activity. So does the 'Hands over the back of a chair' procedure. In the latter case, there should be less unnecessary involvement of the shoulders and an encouragement of greater control yet sensitivity in the hands, through not wrecking all the parts on the way to the extremities, or ruining the total pattern when applied to the particular.

For some time it will be difficult to catch the real-life stimulus and deal with it more appropriately, so applying the principle too directly too soon is asking too much. Often you will be half-way through a movement and become aware of doing something harmful to yourself. You can, of course, go back to the beginning and start again with the greater attention to yourself, but this can become tedious especially as most of us would probably need to do this most of the time at first. Do not make things too difficult for yourself. If you constantly try to catch the real-life situation and find that you cannot, you only give yourself a series of disappointing experiences, and after a while you go off the whole idea of doing anything about yourself, resorting once again to boring exercise programmes which soon pall, or, even more harmfully, to the bottle or to pills. Certainly it is asking too much of the Technique to be able to apply it directly to complex activities, or really difficult situations in the early days, though, as I've suggested before, you can certainly apply it to many trivial but frequently occurring activities to great effect, surprisingly quickly. In time you find that you are applying it to quite difficult and complex activities, though by then they will perhaps not seem so difficult or complex.

What you should do is actually, consciously, give yourself a stimulus to move or do something, rather than try to deal with the real-life situation coming at you from some outside source; then you can inhibit, order and give the right kind of attention to yourself before reacting and carrying out the activity or movement. The movements in the Alexander 'repertoire' are designed to be most effective and bring about the greatest amount of useful improvement over a reasonable period, but any movement can be useful and valuable if approached in this way. The improvement might be imperceptible or quite obvious, but it cannot be so bad as if you had not thought in this way. It might not 'feel' better – though frequently it will, and certainly it will often feel less of an effort – but it is bound to BE better so long as you really think of what the orders mean when you give consent to the movement. As most people are getting worse, not only reinforcing old harmful patterns and bad habits with every reaction and movement, but often adding on extra layers of tension and mis-use, even an apparent slight improvement is a definite and real change in a better direction. It only takes a matter of seconds to think in these terms, and yet each time you do you are allowing for something better to happen, and to do this a dozen or so times a day builds up into a remarkable leap forward, and real progress surprisingly quickly. As Marjory Barlow would say, 'If you move it CAN improve'.

Frequently pupils will come to me and say, 'But it doesn't feel the same when *I* do it'. Of course the teacher has to check just what it is they are doing, but then he or she will need to point out that it does not really matter. What is important is that it is better than when they were not working in this way, better than they would have been if not thinking like this, and probably more valuable as 'real' work than having a lesson.

Work on yourself when you are feeling well; once again it is asking too much to expect instant relief when you are totally wrecked, at least in the earlier days. Usually the time when we do not think we need to work is the best time for consolidation and stabilisation of any improvement, often allowing for another leap forward to a higher level of awareness. Sometimes when you seem 'stuck', you will just be allowing things to settle down again in a new state. It is often a sign that with continued, gentle, regular work you are about to make another breakthrough; perhaps even a bit of extra work at such a time is a good idea, but do not 'end-gain'. You should be content just to be working rather than gaining results, only in this way will you get really worthwhile results. After all it makes life simpler, and, to quote Majory Barlow again, 'Why bother with all the unnecessary worry of trying hard to get it right when all you can do is order'.

Try to apply 'Monkey', continuing the movement as low as necessary. Here, the pupil's head is slightly pulled back and he is bending too much from the lower back, not using his hip joints sufficiently

Often you can avoid a crisis if you have done the work on yourself beforehand, or you can deal with that crisis without it destabilising you so much. Sometimes you look back and think, 'That situation would have wrecked me a few months ago'. Indeed it might not even seem like a crisis but just another situation that can be dealt with reasonably. If you wait for things to go wrong, and only then try applying the principle, you will be past helping yourself, and will not have the requisite stability and confidence needed to cope, asking too much both of the Technique and of yourself.

It is no good thinking once a week, 'Oh heavens, I haven't done my Alexander', and then trying hard to achieve something. *Gentle, regular attention is worth any amount of hard work* which will inevitably be associated with effort and 'doing', all the things that have probably got you into the mess you are trying to get out of. Get used to using all those odd moments in the day which might otherwise be wasted to check the balance and alignment of the body, apply 'monkey' when washing your hands at a low washbasin, cleaning your teeth or picking things up. Be aware of yourself when seated, get your bottom well back in the chair and support the back if necessary. It is all grist to the mill, and encourages the much-needed familiarisation with the new, better state. When you are working long hours or doing something particularly strenuous, get used to stopping frequently, and going back to your orders and a better state of balanced rest. You will find that this will allow you to keep going much longer with much less of a build-up of harmful tension, though it is often the last thing we want to do when we get really involved in some project, but it will allow you to function much more efficiently for much longer periods with consequent improved results.

The combination of pure and applied work is very important. The second without the first is impossible, and the first on its own is a corruption of F.M.'s ideas. Living in some rarefied world of pure Alexander might be very nice but does the work an injustice. Those practitioners and pupils who spend their lives smugly inhibiting, looking faintly superior, as though they have found life's secret, but never getting on with living it, are not, as they imagine, standing apart in a state of desirable detachment or 'non-doing' but have made this aspect of the work an end in itself and are simply in a state of 'nothing doing'. If properly applied it is a highly practical way of living and a better means of coping, but this cannot be achieved without a great deal of pure work on yourself. This is not easy even if the principle is a simple one. We ask people to be in a state of constant awareness, not just in their lessons but in most of their daily life. Certainly in a lesson we ask for every stimulus and movement to be inhibited and the best lessons occur when a pupil is in a well-prepared and ordered state before starting. This in itself is quite demanding and the reason why most lessons are only half to three-quarters of an hour long – it is asking too much of a pupil in the early stages to attend in this way for much longer – but to be so committed in all areas of one's life and to embark upon what amounts to a life sentence is asking a great deal of anyone. You do not HAVE to take it to such a sophisticated level in this all-embracing way but the results will be many and the rewards great if you do. Some pupils think it is so important in their lives that it is worth making quite major sacrifices for. One of my pupils, whilst teaching trainee psychologists at a famous clinic, became so depressed at seeing his students pulling down to the appalling use-level of the patients that he chose to give up his lucrative appointment. Presumably the psychologists were trying to identify with the patients by doing this when it would doubtless have benefited the patients much more to have had examples of good use sitting before them.

This constant attention to yourself can seem like self-absorption and a rather selfish way of going on, if it is not applied, but properly used it becomes a better way of dealing with your activities, relationships, problems and life in general. You are more useful to people if you are in a good state. As a reasonable, stable, human being you can affect your environment for the good, whereas a neurotic, unstable, weak and unreliable person creates havoc all around.

Lastly, do not buy too many clothes during the early period of work. You are quite likely to change shape.

I try to be a true attendant upon grace. Perhaps it will come – perhaps it will not come. Perhaps this quiet yet unquiet waiting is the harbinger of grace, or perhaps it is grace itself. I do not know. But that does not disturb me. In the meantime I have made friends with my ignorance.

Franz Kafka

Questions asked of Alexander teachers

All teachers are frequently asked the same old questions by their pupils and often the answer is 'That's not the right question' or 'It's not like that', but in the earlier stages of learning it is understandable that the pupil will still think in old, familiar terms. Such questions become less frequent as the lessons progress, but nevertheless I will try to deal with a few of the commonest.

How many lessons will I need?

One cannot say. How long is a piece of string? The important point is to bring about the necessary change of direction in your life to allow for progress and improvement. Speed of progress is not so important nor amount of improvement providing it is in the right direction. The change and growth are like those of a flower: we know the direction in which it will go, but usually not the shape or where the petals will be, in what position, at any one time. When pupils learn not to 'end-gain' they appreciate this, and as they work on themselves and find improved ways of dealing with various areas of life this will in itself be so much better than the old way of going on that they will no longer think in such terms. A basic course of lessons to gain sufficient knowledge of the Technique to go on improving on your own will vary wildly depending on many factors. Most pupils will have gained considerable benefits in a dozen or so lessons, but will probably need a few more just to be fully conversant with the basic principles and working methods. To be certain of having made permanent progress yet more lessons might be needed, but these can be spread over a longer period as continuity will no longer be so important. So, it takes as long as it takes, depending on how far you want to take it.

Occasional refresher or booster lessons thereafter are a good idea, depending on how far you wish to go, what the original problems are, and on how much time can be spent working on your own.

Can I teach myself?

In theory 'yes', in practice it is exceedingly difficult. Obviously F.M. taught himself, and his brother A.R., who suffered a crippling accident when thrown from a horse, followed F.M.'s teaching on his own, recovered from his accident and went on to teach the Technique, much of the time in the USA. It was his proud boast that F.M. had never put his hands on him, but he did have his brother to observe and his books to read. But F.M. was a very exceptional man and A.R. was no doubt blessed with the single-mindedness of most of the Alexanders, and had his brother's guidance. We lesser mortals, on the other hand, usually need help. There are those around who claim to have taught themselves, and no doubt by sticking to the principles, however inaccurately or approximately, have made some sort of progress on their own, but with a good teacher to guide them, they would almost certainly have made better progress and gone further. There are 'Teach yourself' books around but some are misleading to say the least. A good teacher can always take you that bit further than you can go on your own, and will prevent you from going up wrong roads and blind alleys, making the whole process more efficient, less time-wasting, more accurate and subtle and altogether less difficult. But whilst I would rarely recommend trying to teach yourself there is no substitute for *working* on yourself.

Can the Technique be taught in groups?

I think not, though you will find many such groups around. The group situation is all right as an introduction to the work, when the basic principles are being explained, or, at the opposite end of the scale, when pupils have had lots of lessons – when in fact they are mostly working on themselves but with a teacher moving around just to check what is going on. Most training courses are in groups but in this situation the students will probably have had many lessons prior to starting training, should know how to work on themselves to some degree, and will be committed to this group work for at least three years on a regular basis, so it is not quite what most people think of as trying to learn the Technique

153

in a group. There is no substitute for the individual attention pupils receive from the one-to-one situation, nor for the experiences gained through a good teacher's handling, which can only be minimal and rarely adequate in a group. Groups who try to apply the principle to other areas, disciplines and activities can, again, at best be only working crudely unless all the members of that group have had a lot of individual work previously and know how to work on themselves.

When will I feel better?

Once again the real answer is 'We don't know'. Frequently quite early lessons will bring about feelings of ease, lightness and well-being, though with some pupils there might even be temporary feelings of discomfort as patterns begin to change and muscles work either for the first time or in different ways. Whilst you might well lose an ache or pain through skilled manipulation from a good teacher, this is not the really important purpose of the work. Of course if you are in great pain and it can be alleviated, then you can more easily attend to the real point of the whole business; it is difficult to give full and proper attention to an improving total pattern in the body if one part is demanding all your attention through constant pain, but here a good teacher will often be able to help. Before you start lessons, you should check with your doctor that you are doing the right thing and that you know as much about your problem as you can.

A major cause of pain in general is mis-use and unnecessary tension so it is essential to deal with this cause. You can deaden and disguise pain with tension and often this will be an understandable reflex reaction. Eventually, however, it will surface or spread in a wider area or worse form, whereupon the temptation will be to create even more tension and mis-use, only to aggravate the problem further. Rather than succumb to this vicious circle, it is better to tackle pain by releasing and working through it, difficult though this may be. It is more likely that the actual cause of the pain will be eradicated by this means and, even if it is not, at least it will not be aggravated unnecessarily nor will there be harmful compensations. The Technique helps to stop the vicious circle by dealing with the mis-use, and creates the best circumstances for the natural healing processes to occur, often in conjunction with all manner of improvements. You cannot grow a new limb if one is missing, but you can make the best of what you have. The relief gained through the release of tension often comes as a new freedom in which you can act more reasonably and begin to take responsibility once again for your own welfare.

It would be foolish to ignore or dismiss the many sorts of treatment available to us for our various ailments, and the Technique cannot always be a substitute for medical attention but, in dealing with our own 'use', we are taking this basic and necessary area into account, which is unlikely to be so in these other approaches.

When will I get things right?

The process is not like that, as the pupil will soon realise. Often you can only know when things are wrong, but by working in the way I have described, you can be sure things will be better, imperceptibly perhaps or dramatically sometimes, even if, for some time your body does not feel so. You do not reach a point of perfection at which everything is right; walking, sitting, standing correctly. Even if you could, it would make life very boring to be in one state all the time with nothing to work towards; and to think in such terms is to set limits on your potential. If you think 'now I've got it' you stop finding out just how far you can go. Life is too complicated to maintain some ideal state. I often tell my pupils that life is there to wreck us and so learning to deal with this challenge can be exciting. We are always, especially if leading a full and busy life, being bombarded by new and difficult stimuli, liable to be knocked off an even keel. Through the Technique we can survive all this without lasting damage and in fact enjoy life more in this knowledge. As things improve you will often be reminded of when things are wrong. Frequently the body protests if you try to force it back into the old harmful ways when it has had some experience of the better ones, and this reminder helps you to be aware and gain more comfort, confidence and ease in the new manner of use.

> Stress is something all living things are subject to just through living, but only human beings could be idiotic enough to load everything against themselves so heavily by choosing a claustrophobic family life founded on a guilt-ridden religion, and living cooped up in a stinking, over-crowded city in which they struggle with everyone else for a sliver of the material benefits of a system based on destructive/aggressive competitiveness.
>
> John Irving

Which muscles do I use?

The mechanical approach is quite wrong. Working things out in this way, wanting to know where the impetus comes from, thinking in terms of positions, levers, pulleys, gravity, angles and muscle-power is never a good idea. By thinking in such terms you are using something you are familiar with as a guide. Learning the Technique should be a journey into the unknown with little reference to past experience; what we are aiming at are new experiences without old limitations. Do not limit yourself, you might get a pleasant surprise and find that you are reaching into completely new areas. How otherwise do great ballet dancers defy gravity? Thinking mechanically is too much like old conventional methods of exercise and like trying to force the whole, complex, psycho-physical mechanism into the role of a machine. We are much more complicated than any machine, and by thinking thus we do not allow for the more difficult areas of mind and feelings that govern everything we do. A knowledge of anatomy is useful to the teacher to back up his work but not essential. F.M. had scant knowledge of such areas, at least in his younger days, and when taken to task for this by certain anatomists his reply was: 'If a knowledge of anatomy is so important, how is it you use your bodies so appallingly?' No amount of anatomical or physiological knowledge can take the place of the hard work essential to learning how to use the body well. All recent anatomical, physiological and neurological research has, however, substantiated Alexander's major theories and this can be a help when you are asked:

How do you know that the Technique works?

The usual answer is 'operational verification'. I always suggest that my pupils do not have to believe a word I say if they so choose, but they should listen carefully and try out what I suggest. If they do they will find that it works. As most of our ideas are quite scientifically based, and in many ways people are more open-minded than they used to be, there is less suspicion around. Also the Technique is not presented as some instant or overnight cure-all fresh from the wilder parts of California. It is hard work and a very strict discipline which has been taught for a century with thousands of living examples of proof that it works.

What about exercising?

As in so many other areas, it's 'not what you do but the way that you do it' that matters most. Unfortunately most people embarking on exercise programmes have no detailed knowledge of the 'how'. Often they are merely exercising their problems and encouraging an unbalanced development. You have only to look at most joggers with their heads pulled back, necks poked forward, chests fixed, breathing constricted, shoulders and elbows pulled back and their backs thrown in to know that they are doing more harm than good. Many people feel they need some sort of exercise however, especially if they are in a particularly sedentary occupation, and this is where 'the way that you do it' comes in. Gentle, symmetrical activities are better than forceful ones. Walking is probably best of all, but cycling (avoiding a dropped-handlebar model, which will encourage the retraction of the head on to the top of the spine and an excessive curve in the spine) and swimming, but preferably not breast stroke (which again produces the same problem with the head – but you will be buoyed up by the water and do not have gravity to contend with so much).

Orthopoedic specialists are constantly having to deal with the ailments of sportsmen, dancers and physical fitness fanatics, and when you ask these people why they indulge in these activities they will often say 'Well, I have to keep fit, don't I?' The penny never seems to drop. Is it not crazy to exercise like a maniac for a short period, only to go off and grossly mis-use yourself for the rest of the day. A feeling of temporary well-being can be encouraged

An example of good use in an athlete

157

by this furious activity. A kind of natural morphine – endorphins – is released in the brain giving an artificial 'high', but there is little proof that such strenuous activities do any lasting good and only too much evidence to the contrary. Of course if you are fanatically interested in some such activity and desperately need to develop huge muscles, encourage enormous stamina, become a ballet dancer or champion squash player, then the choice is yours, but do not imagine for one moment that such activities will encourage better functioning in life generally. They are quite likely to be positively detrimental in this area, whereas even a basic attention to improved use will allow for greatly improved functioning. By even more carefully attending to use, it is as though we are gently and naturally exercising the body in almost everything that we do. You can sit at the office desk comfortably without slumping, even for long periods, also when watching television you can be maintaining length and good use, and likewise in most activities. When you are reasonably secure in the improved manner of use then it can be applied to the sporting activities you enjoy and, even if they are detrimental to some extent, at least you should by

Sports can often encourage misuse: note the jogger's tendency to twist; the gymnast's excessively concave back and braced legs; the cyclist's retracted head, pronounced hump and generally curved spine; and the way the swimmer pulls back his head

then have a means of re-establishing a balanced resting state and undoing any harmful patterns that have been set up.

Am I too old to change?

Not if you really want to. George Bernard Shaw did not even start his lessons until he was eighty. Most important are motivation and the desire to do something about yourself. If children are sent by their parents but cannot themselves see the need, it can be a difficult task for the teacher. You can stimulate them in all sorts of devious ways and they can grow to enjoy the new ways of approaching things, especially as it will all be so different from what their usual teachers ask of them, but it is much easier for both parties if the pupil realises a need. Of course, chronic ailments and the problems of great age can make matters difficult, but old people with quite major problems can achieve apparent miracles through being properly motivated and realising that it is never too late to do something about themselves. Such pupils are often much easier to teach and can gain greater rewards than the reluctant child with apparently trivial problems. On the preventive level it is a good idea to try to interest children, and in an ideal world the principle would be applied at the most basic level of education and from thereon, but often people do not want to know until things go obviously wrong. Not only is there a problem with the unmotivated child who is sent by his parents, but another difficult customer is the pupil sent by the spouse or good friend having been told 'It's just what you need'. Unless they fully appreciate that need, they will either be too lazy in their approach or defy you, as a teacher, to help them. There are many exceptions in these categories, of course, but old age is no barrier to learning if the desire and faculties are there. Even if the problems of old age cannot be cured by the Technique, usually they can be alleviated to some degree, and prevented from becoming much worse.

What about sleeping?

Once you are asleep matters are no longer under your conscious control and so the Technique can only affect them indirectly, but nevertheless sometimes quite noticeably for the better. In the general sorting-out process many pupils find they sleep better as they are much more aware of the build-up of unnecessary tension and can deal with it, and as they get used to the ordering process, they can use that aspect of it which helps calm down the overactive brain. Many insomniacs find great relief, especially if they have got into the habit of disguising their true state with overtension; sometimes this can have been going on and building up for many years, and as they learn how to release that tension they become aware of just how tired they are, and can take appropriate action, i.e. rest or sleep. It is not unknown for a good teacher to bring this about in one or two lessons, but, of course, it will take considerably longer for the pupil to deal with the problem on his own.

One eminent writer and broadcaster who 'hadn't slept properly for twenty years' and used to prop herself up in bed, no doubt in a harmful position, and read all night, came for her first lesson, went home and slept for twenty-four hours. It was as though she suddenly had been made aware of just how tired she actually was.

It is a good idea when in bed to start off by lying on the back in a good balanced resting state, projecting your orders, as this is the easiest way to get rid of some of the tension that has built up during the day. If you then turn on to your side or curl up, it does not matter particularly, but at least try to keep some length in the body – so do not curl tightly or hunch up the shoulders. Sleeping on the tummy is not generally a good idea, even though it is supposed to help with snoring, as it is difficult to keep length in the lower back this way; but if you feel you really need to do this, perhaps when sunbathing, it is advisable to put a cushion or pillow under your tummy so that you do not throw in the lower back. On waking it is not a bad idea to lie on the back for a few minutes and sort yourself out, especially if you have been sleeping in an odd position.

Gradually, as the muscles become re-educated into better patterns, able to release and lengthen again more easily, it actually feels uncomfortable to tighten, jam the head back into the pillow, or hunch the shoulders, and so we tend to prefer a more reasonable lying position. Do not waste money on expensive orthopaedic beds. A firm base giving good support is advisable but one not so hard as to be uncomfortable, and usually a board under an ordinary good mattress will suffice.

Will the Technique help me to stop smoking?

Only indirectly. There is a theory that inhaling smoke gives us a sense of our physical awareness as we breathe more deeply and fill up the lungs. To the ordinarily physically unaware person this experience is unusual and enjoyable. The habit is therefore very difficult to break. However, the Technique should give the pupil a new, better physical awareness that can replace the other and help with overcoming the habit. As the general psycho-physical re-education takes place, with the consequent feelings of improved well-being and greater awareness in many areas, increasing self-confidence and control of habitual responses in all sorts of situations will help the pupil bring a little more common sense to bear on many activities, perhaps even on smoking.

What about diet?

This is a similar problem. We do not make any recommendations in this area as this is not what we are teaching. In any case, with dietary theories changing all the time, how can we? The improvement in controlling habits generally, rather than being controlled by them, will help any desired change in this area, and the ability to choose will inevitably lead to wiser eating patterns. With improved use will go a noticeable improvement in posture which will often obviate the need to slim too radically, and if there seems to be a need to do extra exercise along with a need to diet, then at least there should be a greater awareness of *how* to exercise wisely.

Certainly too much weight is bad if you have a back problem, and some pupils will need to lose weight. It is difficult for teachers to work on really fat pupils as they simply cannot find the bones, and all that weight can wreck the teacher if he or she is not very careful. In this sort of case it is essential that the teacher encourage the pupils to work on themselves and take full responsibility from the outset. Alexander himself ate good quality food but in small quantities, perhaps something we should all do.

How will I know if my teacher is any good?

A very wise question. As in all fields there are those who are good and those who are not so good. F.M. used to say that any Alexander teacher will do you more good than anybody else except a better teacher, but there are many con men and women around in this sort of area, so it is a good idea to check a teacher's credentials. In the UK, at least, most of them have been adequately trained, but there are odd charlatans around who have only been pupils and then set themselves up as teachers, thinking that it is quite easy to yank people's heads up, or whatever it is they imagine is going on. Simple it may seem, but easy it is not. There are professional bodies of practitioners in many countries, governing to some extent the training of student teachers and the behaviour of their members, so it is wise to check this first of all and then perhaps go on recommendation or a teacher's reputation and experience. The training programme for a teacher is usually at least three years long, but a good training course will insist on the student being well-acquainted with the work before embarking on such a course. I would consider that at least one year of regular lessons, and preferably much longer, is essential before beginning to train, as the rate of change experienced during training is so rapid and the difficulties encountered often so great, that unless one is already well on the way, with at least a modicum of basic stability, and thoroughly committed to and trusting the principle, the process at this concentrated level can be disorientating, upsetting and thoroughly terrifying, like any journey into the unknown. It will also, of course, be wonderfully encouraging, enlightening and thrilling.

'The function of an art is to free the intellect from the tyranny of the affects, or, leaning on terms, neither technical nor metaphysical: the function of an art is to strengthen the perceptive faculties and free them from encumbrance. . . .'

Ezra Pound

The teacher has to be both artist and scientist; able to observe, explain, demonstrate and communicate on different levels, frequently all at the same time. He or she must have a keen eye and a sympathetic ear, sometimes needing to be quite devious to bring about a certain experience, but ruthlessly pure in his or her approach. As the teacher/pupil relationship is so close, the teacher must be particularly fastidious with regard to personal hygiene, and a friendly manner would seem to be important. I rather think that really good teachers are born not made.

The teacher's hands are of paramount importance, as they are usually the most direct instrument of communication. It takes a long time to train a teacher to use his or her hands skilfully and they are just part of a general high level of use that the teacher must acquire. I am told that a huge part of the brain governs the hands alone, compared with the rest of the body. It is obviously important to train the hands to be sensitive, accurate, subtle, gentle and highly skilful. Through the hands the teacher is able to assess and check what the pupil is doing and then, with his or her cooperation, bring about the improved experiences needed.

Skilful manipulation, whilst very valuable, is only one part of it however. Getting the pupil to attend in the right way is equally important. In the main, a good teacher should be able to bring about the maximum effect with the minimum of effort, providing the pupil is cooperating in the right way, i.e. inhibiting and ordering. The teacher cannot use excessive effort or he or she will land up in trouble, and it is impossible to do a full day's teaching work in an efficient and subtle manner if his or her own use is not good. Whilst there is no reason why a teacher should be a paragon of virtue, it is important to be a good example of the Technique and able to maintain a reasonably high standard of use throughout most of his or her activities.

There are, of course, lots of exceptions and there is a place for many different kinds of teachers, but I suspect that the teacher who has had the biggest problems often turns out in the end to be the best kind. By undergoing a long period of change and overcoming the many problems along the way, a potential teacher will have had experiences that are greatly valuable in his or her future work. Providing he or she remembers just how long it can take to sort things out, and just how difficult this can be, a teacher is bound to be more sympathetic to pupils' problems. This all takes time and a vast amount of patience. Teachers who were not ready for training or who did not encounter too many difficulties on the way or have not really got to grips with their own problems are unlikely to last long in the profession. I am not suggesting that all pupils will find the process so difficult or long-winded, but a serious teacher cannot be created overnight; it requires a deep commitment to a lot of hard work over many years.

Beware the teacher who does not explain clearly, or who tries to present the work as some mysterious or wondrous answer to all your problems. It is not easy to explain fully in a very concise way, but over a course of lessons a reasonably detailed and clear explanation of the method should emerge and any failure to answer the pupil's questions about the work probably indicates an inadequate teacher. Also beware of the teacher who mixes the Technique with other disciplines, philosophies, exercise or movement-training programmes. There is quite enough to learn for some considerable time just trying to grasp the rudiments of the principle: there are no short cuts or substitutes for the basic, pure hard work and, whilst it is important to learn to apply the ideas, if you try to do this too soon without the basic ground work, you will either be end-gaining or failing to do justice to either the Technique or the area of application.

Finally, the real criteria are: is the teacher teaching the fundamental ideas unique to this technique, those of inhibition and direction, and is he or she teaching you to work on yourself so that you can apply these principles? And a good pupil will be one who does.

Apart from this there is the question of the temperament of both parties. Only you can judge this for yourself, but a few words on the sort of situations that arise in the pupil/teacher-relationship might be useful. For continuity and efficiency it is a good idea to keep to one teacher for at least the first dozen or more lessons, probably longer. Eventually this becomes less important and it can be quite a good idea to experience another approach and have a different pair of hands to inhibit. We easily get used to one way of working and to vary this now and then keeps us on our toes; but at the start too much chopping and changing around only makes for confusion.

A very close working relationship between the teacher and pupil builds up in these early, important lessons, and often the pupil will become quite involved with the teacher on a number of levels as he or she goes through various vivid experiences at the teacher's hands, and the teacher will be professionally concerned for the pupil. A deep trust in the teacher might well develop and many pupils will be greatly influenced by their particular instructor; almost a parent/child situation can arise. When the pupil finds out that the teacher is also vulnerable, and all too human, even being ill now and then, disappointment – even resentment – can set in, especially if the pupil has been at a low ebb and is desperate for an answer to problems. When teachers are also found to have failings, some pupils almost turn on them as if they had in some way let them down. It is therefore perhaps a good idea to make sure that, as a teacher, you do not get too closely involved with your pupils, except in the purely professional sense of teaching them well, so that, eventually, when they have to stand on their own feet, they are able to do so without resentment and with a reasonable stability and trust in the principle and their own ability to apply it.

If the teacher does not teach the pupil to work on him- or herself, disappointment will result from this inability. As teachers we are not therapists, doctors, psychiatrists or gurus and, although pupils will try to cast us in these roles – and indeed good teachers might well have some of the qualities of the above – it should be made clear from the outset that we are here essentially to teach. The opposite situation can also occur: when the teacher resents the pupil no longer needing him or her and, like any fledgling, the pupil needs to fly off on his own, but this should be seen as a good sign and a compliment to the teacher's good teaching. A good teacher will have few problems in these areas but where temperaments and personalities are concerned you can never be totally sure.

Why do Alexander people look so stiff?

If they do look stiff, then they have got hold of the wrong end of the stick. Keeping length certainly, stiff no. Frequently in the early stages of lessons pupils will try too hard and be seen to be fixing into the new alignment. Once you try to keep the improvement going by fixing, however, you have immediately lost it. Although it is understandable that the pupil will want to maintain a better state and will try hard to do this, it must be explained that 'it is not like that' and that making effort in the old way, using old criteria through feeling, and reducing the work to a level of sitting straight or standing correctly is a kind of 'end-gaining' attitude that neglects the all-important 'means whereby' you can improve. As you become more secure and stable in the new better state, you should look better, not peculiar. Of course, if you see a whole group of people who are not pulling down, collapsing, hunching, twisting or fixing, it will probably be quite noticeably different even to the untrained eye, but if you want to change, then by definition you are going to be different, so you cannot be expected to fit into what other people think of as being acceptable. What we find aesthetically pleasing is very subjective. We are conditioned by advertising, the media and even great art into thinking certain states are desirable. Film stars, pin-ups and fashion magazines are constantly parading before us types and conditions to which we are supposed to aspire, but it does not take much thought to realise how often fashions change and the example we are supposed to emulate one year is soon thought of as laughable. The boyish figure of a 'Twiggy' is soon replaced by the more curvaceous Jerry Hall; the lanky Garbo gives way to a luscious

Ideas of beauty are many and various and have little to do with how well we use ourselves

Monroe; the generous fullness of a Rubens must be curbed and constricted into the 'genre' respectability of the burgher's wife; and the Michelangelo ideal of David for the Lowry matchstick man. The androgynous male model of the Sixties gives way to the super-butch muscle-man of the Eighties, even the Tarzans of yesteryear seem puny alongside the incredible hulks of today. Too often we are presented with these examples of the mis-used, excessively curved, over-muscled or anorexically-thin, so we need to change our criteria and learn to appreciate good use, balance, symmetry, good alignment, freedom and stability. The appreciation of our own improved use will help us delight in these rare examples. It is too depressing constantly to be reminded of the mis-use all around us: we begin to wonder how some people manage to move at all, so we often have to ignore this, attend to our own manner of use and appreciate the beautiful neck, the pleasing line of the shoulders, the well-modulated voice, or the easy walk when we do occasionally encounter them.

Is it like Yoga?

I don't know much about Yoga, but I'm sure there are some similarities and overlapping areas, as there are with so many other disciplines, meditation, Zen, body-awareness techniques, and suchlike. In the east where Yoga is taught from earliest childhood and becomes a way of life, then a harmony of mind and body is often achieved, similar to that which the Alexander Technique aims to develop. In the west where Yoga, in its various forms, is often badly taught, I sometimes think it does as much harm as good. Certainly many of the back problems we see are caused by people doing Yoga, probably incorrectly. Unlike Yoga, the Technique does not expect you to exercise. The movements involved are a practical repertoire which can be used in everyday situations to encourage more efficient functioning, not something to be done separately for the rest of life. They require a great deal of thought and attention, but are in no sense a 'cutting off' from the outside world, even when a desirable state of detachment is achieved. The Technique is unique, with its own essential elements.

What should I wear for my lessons?

As I suggested before, it is a good idea to wear something comfortable and unrestricting. Whilst it is important to learn to use yourself well in any situation and wearing any kind of clothes, however crazily fashionable, it makes matters difficult for both teacher and pupil if skirts and trousers are too tight. Too much bare flesh and the teacher tends to stick to it and is unable to manipulate effectively, so singlets are not a good idea, better something that covers the shoulders. High heels are obviously undesirable and bad for the back. After a few lessons pupils tend to realise that certain garments are better than others, both generally and for their lessons, and they often take this into account when buying clothes. Even if they do choose to wear something that encourages mis-use, at least they will be aware of this, and it will not be comfortable, perhaps worn only for shorter periods when to be fashionable is important. To get the greatest benefit from a lesson it is a good idea for the teacher tactfully to point out these things fairly early on, but it is not necessary to buy special clothes.

Should I get a special chair?

It is what *you* are doing to yourself that matters, and I am rather against blaming *things* for our problems. There is no chair that is perfect for everybody, and if there were you could not carry it around with you everywhere you went. If you sit at a desk all day long, then obviously it is a good idea to have a chair which suits your size and needs, and supports your back reasonably. Specially designed chairs might suit certain people, but I think a lot of these are a bit of a confidence trick. Rather, as with clothes, one chooses more wisely in time: an upright chair of a suitable size with a straight back, or – if relaxing in an easy-chair or on a sofa – then a cushion or two to give support to the back where necessary.

Can anyone learn the Alexander Technique?

To some degree, I suppose, yes. Even the youngest, stupidest, or most afflicted can be given a good experience at the hands of a skilled teacher, and can benefit. But this is only one aspect of the Technique, and a minor one at that. To understand the principles and to be able to apply them does require a certain amount of intelligence and attention. However, some very intelligent pupils who question everything and complicate matters are often the most difficult to teach, since they see problems where they do not exist, or are unable to give the right kind of simple, direct attention to the matters in hand. They can also be stimulating to teach, but quite frustrating too, and progress can be slow.

Whilst one does not want slavish obedience, the sort of pupil who listens carefully and goes away to give it a try will often improve most quickly. This does not require a high degree of intelligence, just a modicum of common sense, and, as with elderly pupils, strong motivation. Even some apparently quite unintelligent people make spectacular progress, as trying what is suggested quite simply and working on themselves makes sense to them. Perhaps it is just a different kind of intelligence, not the usually accepted academic or intellectual sort. Hyper-active children will be difficult, probably impossible to teach until the hyper-activity is sorted out. Pupils who fall asleep on the teacher, not uncommon, are also difficult, as are the lazy, and those deeply involved in other disciplines who try to see the Technique in the same terms. Those who dabble in all sorts of areas rarely have the application to learn properly, but perhaps the most difficult category that one meets is the highly neurotic type. They cannot get their minds off their problems, possibly even enjoy them too much to want really to change, and are reluctant to attend to the means whereby they can deal with them. Which brings us into the realms of mental health.

Can it help with mental problems?

Certainly. As Alexander teachers we are dealing with the whole person, unlike many approaches to mental health where they are only trying to sort out the psychological state. Psycho-analysis and psychotherapy imply a division of the self. After a century or more of this approach we do not seem to have progressed too far: certainly there seem to be more mental problems around than ever before. As many intelligent people are more and more reluctant to take drugs, maybe a different approach is needed, one in which an awareness of the patient's physical as well as mental state is considered. As we know rather more about the physical, perhaps this is the area that should first be sorted out, or at least emphasised, although in our lessons we do not divorce the two.

If you can persuade a mentally disturbed patient to come for regular lessons, then you have the chance to communicate feelings of coordination, ease, and well-being, which will, in many cases, allow the patient to listen and think more clearly. As we sort out the use of the psycho-physical mechanism, the improved sensory awareness, whereby the patient is more in tune with his or her real state, will allow for more direct communication. In any thereapy or analysis, information communicated through an agitated, disturbed, uncoordinated, mis-used mechanism is of dubious value. Sort out that mechanism and the rewards thereby obtained in the areas of greater self-control, ease, well-being, calmness and so on will often make the therapy seem unnecessary. Whilst knowledge might be desirable in many ways, it will not presuppose a cure, and, as I have pointed out, might well be of a questionable nature. I suggest that relief gained from improved use might often be more helpful to a patient than insight through delving into the past and the psyche. Even at the simplest level everyone knows how much better we feel mentally when we feel well physically, are properly rested, functioning efficiently and so on.

It is generally recognised that anxiety and muscle tension go hand in hand. Posture will often give away the mood of the patient, the depressed body, for example, indicating the depressed mind. Improve the posture and you can alter the mood. Even if the posture is not actually caused by the mood it can create the mood.

Alexander wrote: 'The majority of people have developed a manner of use of themselves which is constantly exerting a harmful influence not only upon their functioning but also upon their manner of reaction. We should be able to see that this wrong use can be a source of individual failings, peculiarities, wrong ideas and ills of all kinds, as well as that inward unrest and unhappiness which is evident in the social life of to-day.' He suggested that all kinds of phobias and mental problems beset us because we are in a poor state of psycho-physical well-being, vulnerable to them because we are unable to react to the situation in a reasonable manner.

If the mental problem has a physical cause, then the answer to that problem is bound to lie to some extent in improving the physical side of things. No doubt there are certain physical types who are predisposed to certain problems, so again it is important that they be made aware of their physical well-being and know how to maintain it through good use. As pupils learn to control their means of reaction and deal more appropriately with each stimulus, they can give themselves a better experience, and lots of good experiences can make for greater stability and happiness.

In the Alexander lesson the change that takes place will be at a much deeper level than that gained through verbal communication. Unlike Freud, who was so convinced of the power of words, perhaps Jung gets nearer the Alexander idea of 'self' as a concept which accounts for the totality, wholeness of experience, and completeness of the person.

A personal story

At the start of this book I suggested that too personal an approach was limiting and did not do the work full justice, so I have tried to remain general and objective, sticking to a description of the principles and practical procedures involved in learning, teaching and applying the Technique. I have tried to keep to the basic areas discovered and taught by Alexander himself and passed on directly by the teachers he himself trained, whilst backing up his theories with recent discoveries and developments. The fundamental principles, hard work and practical procedures involved, without which there is no Technique, are simple if not easy, and I have endeavoured to keep my account as simple as possible, without over-simplifying, and yet to describe some of the more difficult areas to be encountered.

The experiences gained by the individual in the lessons can be vivid, illuminating, uncomfortable, revolutionary, interesting and enlightening to those concerned, but they are not necessarily always applicable or relevant to the next person, and if he or she is led to believe certain experiences will definitely be forthcoming he or she might well be disappointed and hindered from finding out how helpful the work can be.

However, teachers are frequently asked how they themselves found out about the Technique and why they continued in the work. As a final note I would like to touch briefly on this, but emphasising what I think to be the less personal aspects which can be appreciated more generally as lessons that many of us must learn.

Whilst on tour in the original Drury Lane production of *Camelot*, playing Mordred the villain of the piece, I was involved in a serious car accident. Fortunately I chose a spot conveniently near an excellent new intensive care unit, which managed to keep me alive until I was shipped off to a chest and heart hospital for Christmas and major surgery. After this and a surprisingly short period of recuperation, I was able to rejoin the show, an aim that had probably kept me going throughout, though, as it happened, it was perhaps something I should not have done. Cutting out the dancing, and singing with an oddly husky new voice, I managed to complete the rest of the tour, even though in considerable pain. A kind of delayed shock or damage to the nervous system then

172

seemed to take hold, resulting in paralysis, swelling of most of the joints, acute and constant pain and apparent epileptic fits.

It never rains . . . and at this time I was also experiencing many emotional and financial problems. If I spent about twenty hours at a time in bed, even though I could not sleep, and had frequent hot baths, I could just manage to struggle to the corner shop for the basic necessities of life. On one of these sorties I bumped into a fellow actor with whom I'd been appearing in the West End a year or two before. His look of horror told me that I was not disguising my problems very well and when told what was wrong he said, 'Alexander Technique! Can't explain it, just go!' Having tried everything else – numerous specialists, endless drugs, drink – and still getting nowhere, I had nothing to lose. Dr Barlow's reaction was, 'We might just be able to help you'. This seemed to be one of the more sensible and honest approaches I had so far encountered from the medical profession, even though I was totally sceptical, and completely mystified about what I was letting myself in for.

After a month or so of regular lessons, most days, I was improving dramatically, with far less pain and swelling, and was able to nip in the bud any fits that were about to develop by 'putting myself down' on the floor and sorting myself out in some sort of fashion, no doubt still rather crudely, but nevertheless effectively. I still had little idea of what was going on, but knew that things were better. Perhaps in my rather acute state I was unable to take in the basic ideas behind the lessons and would often wonder, rather tetchily, why I was being told to free my neck when the pain was in my arms and legs. With the encouragement, care, indeed love of my teacher, I persisted in spite of the odd set-back, finding I could cope somehow with numerous very difficult situations – in fact now and then I seemed to be coping with all sorts of things in a better way than I did before all these recent problems had arisen. One of the first, rather trivial, instances of this was going into a shop to buy something; they did not have exactly what I wanted, and the skilful sales-person was trying to sell me something similar which I did not really want. Previously I would have been easily brow-beaten into buying this, not wishing to seem difficult or fussy, but on this occasion I firmly refused, smiled and walked out feeling ten feet tall. Where was all this strange new self-confidence coming from – surely not merely from a new strength in surviving all the past year's horrors? This seemed to be the real me whom I had not seen in many years. Usually I would go along with things, then bitterly resent my acquiescence at leisure, despising myself for my weakness.

Some weeks after my lessons started I was to play a good part in a Shakespeare play with a very star-studded cast. It was to open at an international festival in repertoire with another play. This necessitated a complicated rehearsal schedule with a difficult, sadistic, flappable, neurotic director and his decidedly unpleasant sarcastic assistant. After a surprising success we toured the play abroad, brought it into London's West End for a sell-out season, made a film version of it, and with one of the leading actors I was asked to do my scenes as a guest on a television show. This all involved months of travelling and constant re-rehearsing to adapt to different types of theatre and studio. Fortunately the film-star leading-man and the producer were pleasant and easy to work with but, even more important, was the help I got from the Technique. Somehow, by working on myself crudely but regularly I was surviving all this chaos, and even when in pain was able to cope, in fact, rather better than when I had been supposedly well, not to mention getting some of the best reviews!

As I could not afford both singing lessons and Alexander lessons I had to drop the former but found to my astonishment that my voice was better than it had ever been. The curious huskiness experienced after the accident had gone and a new lower resonance and wider range had developed. For the first time in my life since being aware of such matters I did not feel that I had artificially and constrictingly to drop my voice from the rather high-pitched nasality that had been usual up to this point. It seemed that I had found the right placing for the voice without even directly thinking about it.

What was more, I was not experiencing the frequent bouts of depression I had come to expect as a part of life, even though I still had many good reasons to be depressed from time to time. My bad temper seemed to be cured, perhaps it had been caused by the frustration which also seemed to have gone now that I was getting to work on my life. Certain other recurring problems had also disappeared, the twice-yearly, at least, skin rashes which no one could explain, the leg which twitched and juddered as I sat nervously trying to please. The catarrh which I had come to accept as a fact of life after several years had gone, also the acute pain in my feet which had been diagnosed in the Air Force as rheumatism, excusing me from wearing boots. The curious lumps on my feet I had put down to wearing sloppy shoes as a child had disappeared as had the general rather rheumaticky feelings of creaking, cracking and aching which I was sure were caused by a childhood spent frequently under canvas, or getting soaked each evening at the local rowing club and subsequently living in a damp basement flat.

Within a month or so I seemed to have gained an inch in height and my waist was down from 32 inches to 28 inches even though I had not lost any weight, and my friends were remarking that I actually had a neck after all. Of course all of these things did not happen immediately. It was months before I realised some of the changes had taken place – no doubt I was too preoccupied with my more recent and dramatic problems and the relief I was now experiencing – but I was beginning to see that not only were my lessons dealing with the recent damage from the car accident but with a whole lifetime of mis-use up to that point. It was as though my body had said after the crash: 'That's it, the last straw, I can't take any more, I'm giving up.' Now the real work was to begin, a glorious life sentence, not just dealing with the pain and paralysis and problems of the moment, but a thoroughgoing sorting-out process dealing with a lifetime's bad habits and entrenched attitudes.

Looking back I could see that what I had put up with for years and had come to think of as a normal part of living and getting older did not have to be, and in fact could be changed. I would look back at old photographs of this rather collapsed youth, pulling down madly on one side, obviously depressed but smiling bravely through it all and desperately trying to cope with life. But now a new self-confidence was emerging and a distinct feeling that, for the first time that I could recall, my destiny was much more in my own hands. I no longer felt like a character in a Greek tragedy, but like someone who could act positively and consciously control hitherto unexpected areas of his life. What I most liked about this new approach was that it was the first thing that had ever really made sense in my life. It depended most of all on me and me alone. There are few things in life that we can do anything about directly, but this is no reason not to deal with the area we *can* affect, our own lives, and sort out the things that can be changed. Realising that you are not necessarily totally hide-bound by your background and programming, and knowing that you can eventually master your habits instead of them controlling you, is a great relief. To have a choice where before you seemed to have none is a great luxury – even if, sometimes, you choose foolishly, at least you are not now deluding yourself. Having a means of facing the unknown in the knowledge that whatever is flung at you can be dealt with to the best of your ability seems to me to be a great hope for mankind and an immensely practical way of facing the future. Discovering yourself can be painful, but also very rewarding. Unless you face up to this journey into the unknown, how can you progress, knowing that everything you ever thought and did was to some extent suspect? We are our past but that does not mean it has to colour and influence the future adversely. We cannot deny it, but we can at least learn to recognise it honestly and make it a useful lesson for dealing with the future.

'Man will begin in earnest to harmonise his own being. He will aim at bringing higher precision, purposefulness, economy and consequently beauty into the movements of his own body at work, on the march, at play. He will desire to master the half-conscious and unconscious processes of his own organism . . . and he will seek . . . to subordinate them to control reason and will. . . .'

Trotsky

Further reading

F.M. Alexander, *Man's Supreme Inheritance*, 1910
   Constructive Conscious Control of the Individual, 1923
   The Use of the Self, 1932
   The Universal Constant in Living, 1942
Wilfred Barlow, *The Alexander Principle*, 1973
   (ed.), *More Talk of Alexander*, 1978
W.H. Sheldon, *Varieties of Human Physique*, 1940
David Garlick (ed.), *Proprioception, Posture and Emotion*, 1986
W.G. Walter, *The Living Brain*, 1953

For further information about the technique or teachers contact The Society of Teachers of the Alexander Technique (STAT), 20 London House, 266 Fulham Road, London SW10 9EL
Tel: 0171-351 0828   Fax: 0171-352 1556
E-mail: enquiries@stat.org.uk   Internet: www.stat.org.uk